P9-CRA-115

ANTON CHEKHOV

Uncle Vanya

translated from the Russian by
MICHAEL FRAYN

with commentary and notes by
NICK *and* NON WORRALL

Bloomsbury Methuen Drama
An imprint of Bloomsbury Publishing Plc

BLOOMSBURY
LONDON · NEW DELHI · NEW YORK · SYDNEY

Bloomsbury Methuen Drama
An imprint of Bloomsbury Publishing Plc

Imprint previously known as Methuen Drama

50 Bedford Square	1385 Broadway
London	New York
WC1B 3DP	NY 10018
UK	USA

www.bloomsbury.com

BLOOMSBURY, METHUEN DRAMA
and the Diana logo are trademarks of Bloomsbury Publishing Plc

This translation of *Uncle Vanya* first published in 1987 by Methuen London Ltd
This edition first published in the United Kingdom in 2005 by Methuen Publishing Ltd
Reprinted by Bloomsbury Methuen Drama 2010, 2011, 2012, 2013, 2014

Original work entitled *Diadia Vania*

© Michael Frayn 1988, 1991
Commentary and notes © Nick and Non Worrall 2005

British Library Cataloguing-in-Publication Data
A catalogue record for this book is available from the British Library.

ISBN: PB: 978-0-4137-7471-2

Library of Congress Cataloging-in-Publication Data
A catalog record for this book is available from the Library of Congress.

Series: Student Editions

Contents

Anton Chekhov: 1860–1904

1860 Born, the grandson of a serf and third son of the merchant grocer Pavel Yegorovich Chekhov and his wife Yevgeniya Yakovlevna Morozova, in Taganrog, a small southern port on the Sea of Azov, where he spends his first nineteen years.

1868 Enters the local *gimnaziya* or high school, where he acquires a reputation as a practical joker and is known as 'bomb-head' because of the overdeveloped size of his cranium.

1876 His father, bankrupt, flees from Taganrog concealed beneath a mat at the bottom of a cart. The family follow him to Moscow, leaving Chekhov behind to complete his schooling. Chekhov writes a short (2–3 pages) 'absurd' play, called *A Forced Declaration or The Sudden Death of a Horse, or The Magnanimity of the Russian People.*

1878 He writes a full-length play, and a vaudeville, *Why the Hen Clucks*, both now lost. The play, *Bezotsovshchina* (Fatherless/Without Patrimony) may be the one which later resurfaced, and is generally known as *Platonov*.

1879 Having completed his education, Chekhov moves to Moscow to join his family, now impoverished and living in a red-light district. He enters the medical faculty of Moscow University where he studies for the next five years.

1880 Begins contributing humorous stories to minor magazines under the pen-name, Antosha Chekhonte. His first short stories are published in the tenth issue of the magazine *Strekoza* (The Dragonfly).

1880 Chekhov writes for Moscow and St Petersburg comic
–87 magazines under various pseudonyms, 'A Doctor without Patients', 'A Man without a Spleen', 'My Brother's Brother', and others.

1881 He offers a full-length play to the Moscow Maly Theatre which is rejected. Presumed lost, a play is discovered in 1920, without a title, but containing plot elements which resemble those of the rejected work. It is most usually known as *Platonov*, after the play's central character. Because of its inordinate length, the play is usually acted in adapted or abbreviated versions – the most famous being Michael Frayn's *Wild Honey* (1984).

1884 Chekhov qualifies as a doctor and begins practising in the Moscow regions of Zvenigorod and Voskresensk – the start of a sporadic second career which, over the years, brings him much hard work and little income. Describing the relationship between his work as a doctor and that as a writer, he compares them to those between a man and his wife and a man and his mistress, respectively. His first collection of stories, *Fairy Tales of Melpomene*, is published, as is a three-page 'terrible-awful-disgraceful desperate t-r-r-rragedy', *Dishonourable Tragedians and Leprous Dramatists*. A 'dramatic study in one act', *On The High Road*, is rejected by the censor as 'a gloomy and sordid play'. He begins to show first signs of the tubercular condition which was to end his life twenty years later.

1885 Makes his first trip to St Petersburg where he meets and befriends Alexey Suvorin, millionaire proprietor of the newspaper *Novoye vremya* (The New Time), a man of reactionary views who has a concession on all the railway bookstalls in Russia.

1886 Begins writing for *Novoye vremya*. His second collection of short stories, *Motley Tales*, is published. He also writes two short one-acters – *Swan Song* and *On the Harmfulness of Tobacco*.

1887 First production of a full-length play, *Ivanov*, given on 19 November at the Korsh Theatre in Moscow. Despite only four rehearsals 'the play had a substantial success' with curtain calls after each act including one, following Act Two, for the author himself. The production was also hissed. According to Chekhov, the second performance '. . . didn't go badly . . . Again there were curtain calls after Act Three (twice) and after Act Four, but no hisses this time' (letters to his brother, Alexander, dated 20 and 24 November 1887).

1888 Writes a long short story, 'The Steppe', which appears in one of the prestigious 'thick journals' *Russkaya mysl'* (Russian Thought) and which marks a change in Chekhov's attitude to his fiction writing, thanks largely to an appreciative letter from the literary critic, D. V. Grigorovich. Henceforth, Chekhov will write fewer stories and, generally, longer and more substantial ones. This year also sees the appearance of his best-known and most performed one-act 'jokes' – *The Bear* and *The Proposal*. At the première of the first, a samovar bursts on stage and scalds one of the actors. The Russian Academy awards Chekhov the Pushkin prize for a book of short stories, *In the Twilight*.

1889 Chekhov's full-length play, *The Wood Demon*, strongly influenced by Tolstoyan ideas, opens at the Abramova Theatre in Moscow but closes after only three performances. It will later reappear, in revised form, as *Uncle Vanya*. He writes two more short plays, *A Tragedian in Spite of Himself* and the more extended *The Wedding*.

1890 Sets out on a journey in unsprung carts over unsurfaced roads, as well as by train and steamer, to the convict settlement on the island of Sakhalin off Russia's eastern seaboard. The journey takes from 21 April to 11 July. Once there, Chekhov conducts a census of some 10,000 convicts, averaging 160 interviews a day as part of a three-month medical/statistical survey which includes the examination of living conditions among convicts and exiles, looking at school and library provision, etc. He also makes travel notes which are written up as nine articles for *Novoye vremya* and which become the basis of the documentary work, *The Island of Sakhalin*, published in 1895. He leaves Siberia on 13 October and returns by sea via Hong Kong (where he admires British colonial rule) and Ceylon (where he admires the beauty of the women), arriving in Odessa via the recently opened Suez Canal on 1 December.

1891 His one-act play *The Anniversary* staged. Makes his first trip to Western Europe in the company of Suvorin.

1892 He purchases an estate near Moscow, Melikhovo (now a Chekhov museum, as is his residence-cum-surgery in Moscow), where he and the remainder of his family move. During the course of this and the following year, Chekhov immerses himself in the struggle against the effects on the local population of famine and cholera. He also helps to build schools, plants fruit trees, cultivates fir, pine, larch and oak, grows flowers, stocks fishponds, and runs the estate as a self-supporting commune growing its own cereal and vegetables. His medical 'diocese' covers 26 villages. One of his best-known short stories, 'Ward 6', is published in November.

1894 His health worsens but, despite this, he travels to Europe again in the company of Suvorin.

1895 Chekhov's fame as a writer spreads. He meets Tolstoy for the first time.

1896 Sponsors the construction of a primary school in nearby Talezh. *The Seagull* is premièred unsuccessfully at the Alexandrinsky Theatre, St Petersburg. Chekhov vows never to write another play.

1897 Sponsors construction of a primary school in the neighbouring village of Novosyolki. Suffers a violent lung haemorrhage while dining with Suvorin and is diagnosed as suffering from tuberculosis. He is also plagued by piles, gastritis, migraine, dizzy spells, and palpitations of the heart (not unlike the comic protagonist, Lomov, in his one-act 'joke' *The Proposal*). A collection of his plays is published which includes *Uncle Vanya*.

1897 –98 Wintering in Nice for his health, he becomes interested in the Dreyfus case and takes Zola's side in defence of the French officer. Relations cool with the rather anti-semitic Suvorin.

1898 Has a villa built in Yalta on the Black Sea (now a Chekhov museum) where weather conditions are better suited for his illness. Following the opening of the Moscow Art Theatre in October 1898, *The Seagull* is given its second, successful, première in December, produced by Stanislavsky and Nemirovich-Danchenko and with Olga Knipper as Arkadina and Stanislavsky as Trigorin.

1899 Sells Melikhovo and moves permanently to Yalta. Also sells the copyright on all his works, past, present and future, to the St Petersburg publisher, A. F. Marks, for 75,000 roubles. *Uncle Vanya* staged with tremendous success by the Moscow Art Theatre on 26 October, with Knipper as Yelena and Stanislavsky as Astrov. Chekhov begins corresponding with Knipper, whom he had admired at a rehearsal of *Tsar Fedor* in 1898 and whom he is to marry in 1901. One of his best-known short stories, 'Lady with Lapdog', is published. Having corresponded with Gorky, Chekhov meets him for the first time and is instrumental in getting the Art Theatre to perform Gorky's plays *The Merchant Class* and *The Lower Depths*.

1899 Edits and publishes his *Complete Works* in eleven volumes.
–1902
1900 Elected to honorary membership of the Academy of Sciences. Works on *Three Sisters* with members of the Moscow Art Theatre in mind. Winters in Nice.
1901 *Three Sisters* premièred at the Art Theatre on 31 January with Knipper as Masha and Stanislavsky as Vershinin. A qualified success. On 25 May he marries Knipper and honeymoons in south-east Russia. Meetings with Leo Tolstoy, Maxim Gorky, Ivan Bunin and Alexander Kuprin.
1902 Resigns from the Academy of Sciences in protest at Gorky's expulsion from that institution for his radical beliefs.
1903 Second edition of his *Complete Works* published. Despite worsening health, he works on his final play, *The Cherry Orchard*, again with specific Moscow Art Theatre actors in mind.
1904 Première of *The Cherry Orchard* on 17 January. Chekhov is taken seriously ill in the spring. He and Knipper leave for the health resort of Badenweiler in the Black Forest area of Germany, where he dies on 2 July. His last words are a request for champagne. His body is brought by rail to Moscow in a wagon for frozen goods marked 'Oysters' and, on 9 July, is interred in the cemetery of the Novodevichy Monastery, where many of Russia's great writers lie.

Plot

The play is set some time towards the end of the nineteenth century
on the Voinitsky country estate to which Aleksandr Serebryakov, a
retired university professor, has moved with his youthful second
wife, Yelena, to take up residence in a large house with twenty-six
rooms. For the past twenty-five years, the estate has been managed
by his deceased first wife's brother, Ivan Voinitsky (known as
Uncle Vanya), and latterly, by his own daughter (Vanya's niece)
Sonya who, since her father's acquisition of a second wife, seems
to have been living on the estate, with Vanya acting as a kind of
surrogate parent. Vanya has willingly undertaken the management
of the estate out of respect for the professor's position and
learning and what he has believed to be his worldly fame – for a
token remuneration of five hundred roubles a year. However, while
the professor has actually been living with them, Vanya has
become increasingly disillusioned; all he now sees is a decrepit old
man afflicted with gout and other ailments, married to an absurdly
young wife to whom Vanya would have proposed himself some
ten years previously but let the chance slip. The professor now
symbolises for Vanya the waste of his own life, sacrificed for the
sake of a nonentity, an intellectual pygmy and a domestic tyrant.

As if in revenge, Vanya seeks to declare his love to Yelena at
every possible opportunity, much to her irritation. Her presence on
the estate has also attracted the attention of a local landowner and
medical practitioner, Dr Astrov, who has been summoned to
attend Serebryakov and who exploits these opportunities to be in
Yelena's presence, neglecting his more mundane medical duties.
This may be a repetition of comparable behaviour over two
consecutive winters eleven years previously during the lifetime of
the professor's first wife, the reasons for which are never fully
explained; Astrov might either have been attending to her as a
patient or he might have been similarly attracted to her. Sonya has
been in love with him for the past six years and admires him for
his ecological enthusiasms but Astrov, who has been a regular
monthly visitor, is not her suitor. Instead, he finds here a peaceful
haven away from his humdrum bachelor existence and the squalor

of a daily life spent tending his uncouth peasant patients. He has even been given a space of his own in Vanya's estate office-cum-bedroom for his hobby, ecological map-making.

Other residents of the estate include the professor's mother-in-law, Maria Vasilyevna, a staunch admirer of her son-in-law, who spends most of her time aping his intellectual pursuits by browsing through learned pamphlets in which she scratches marginal notes. The other two permanent residents are Marina and Telegin. Marina is an elderly domestic servant, referred to by almost everyone as 'Nanna', who has firm religious beliefs; Telegin is an impoverished, good-natured former landowner, whose wife abandoned him for another after their wedding night, on account, he says, of his pockmarked face and unprepossessing appearance. He is also Sonya's godfather, an inveterate guitar-strummer, and lives on the estate's charity.

Chekhov's description of the action as taking place 'on Serebryakov's estate' gives rise to some confusion in Act Three when Vanya, furious at the professor's intention to sell the property, declares that it is not his to dispose of as it belongs to his daughter Sonya – a fact with which the professor agrees, declaring that he would not sell it without her consent. It emerges during the course of the action that the estate was originally bought as a dowry for Sonya's late mother, Vera Petrovna Serebryakova (née Voinitskaya), by Vera's now deceased father, a privy councillor and Maria Vasilyevna's husband. It was purchased from Telegin's uncle, which may account for the fact that Telegin himself, now apparently propertyless, lives on the estate. When Vera married Serebryakov she came into the estate but appears to have shared her husband's preference for city life in so far as they seem to have spent little time in the country, apart from the two winters eleven years earlier. The estate has been left in charge of Vera's brother, Vanya, who had renounced his rights to the property in favour of his sister at the time of the original purchase, which was 25,000 roubles short of the asking price, the sum being carried over as a debt which Vanya has succeeded in paying off over a period of ten years. Since Serebryakov only came into possession of the estate by virtue of his first wife's demise, he only has a life interest in it, the title belonging in law to his daughter, Sonya.

Chekhov is very specific about the ages of some of the characters and we can deduce the age of others from what is said

about them. So Vanya is forty-seven, Yelena is twenty-seven and
Astrov appears to be about thirty-seven. Sonya's age is uncertain
and it is not clear how young the professor's first wife was when
she married or how old she was when she died or what the cause
of her death was; nor is it clear how long Serebryakov and Yelena
have been married. The duration of the action is equally unspecific
but seems to begin on a sultry afternoon in June, then, in Act
Two, enters the haymaking season (which would suggest July) and
continues into September the same year, with the afternoon of Act
Three being followed by the evening of the same day in Act Four.
How long the professor and his wife have been living on the estate
is unclear. Astrov is described in Act One as having visited the
estate three times since Yelena has been there, so we can surmise
that they have been living there for at least a month before the
play's action commences.

Act One
The play opens in the estate grounds on a sultry summer
afternoon. Astrov has driven some eighteen miles in response to a
letter from Yelena informing him that her husband is unwell, only
to find that the patient refuses to see him. He is discovered talking
to Marina in a general way about time and the way life changes
people, including himself, into oddities and eccentrics. He describes
the awful living conditions of the peasantry and recalls a patient
who died on the operating table. He wonders whether people of a
future generation, one or two hundred years hence, will spare a
thought for those currently living. Vanya enters, looking
dishevelled after a midday nap, but wearing a smart tie. He
complains that the whole routine of estate life has been disrupted
since the arrival of the professor and his wife, a sentiment with
which Marina concurs.

Serebryakov, Yelena, Sonya and Telegin return from a stroll and
all exit into the house apart from Telegin. In conversation with
Astrov, Vanya admits to being jealous of Serebryakov's success
with women and is contemptuous of his intellectual achievements
and lack of fame, as well as being fairly scathing about his own
mother. Yelena, Sonya and Maria Vasilyevna emerge from the
house and join in the desultory round of talking and tea-drinking.
Vanya rails against wasting his life for his convictions, before he
declares that the weather is perfect for hanging oneself. Marina

expresses concern about the fate of some young chicks who have
wandered off and might be attacked by crows. Then a workman
arrives to summon Astrov to the factory. While waiting for a glass
of vodka to be brought him before leaving, Astrov makes a speech
in favour of ecological preservation and speaks of contributing to
the happiness of people a thousand years hence through the work
he puts into the orchard and nursery on his own estate. Sonya has
prefaced this with a similar speech showing how she has taken
Astrov's views to heart.

  With Astrov's departure, Vanya (for the first time in the play
but not, we imagine, for the first time) makes verbal overtures to
Yelena who responds with embarrassment and irritation. Her
reaction seems to epitomise her high-minded sentiments about the
virtues of loyalty, integrity and unselfishness in human affairs
which, embodying them herself, she feels have been replaced in
others by 'a demon of destruction'. The act concludes with Telegin
strumming a polka and Maria Vasilyevna making marginal notes,
a cameo which anticipates the conclusion of the play itself.

Act Two
The action takes place in the dining-room on a stiflingly hot night
between the hours of 12 and 2 a.m., with a thunderstorm brewing.
Yelena is sitting up with Serebryakov, who is suffering from either
gout or rheumatism. The sounds of a watchman patrolling the
estate can be heard through an open window. Serebryakov self-
pityingly complains about pains in his legs and the fact that his
old age makes him repulsive. Yelena shows signs of irritation and
impatience with her husband, who declares that he has a right to
his egotism, misses the fame and activity of his pre-retirement
existence and regrets their move to the country. He inveighs
against his idiotic mother-in-law and the fact that they are now
living in the middle of nowhere; he wants respect from others in
his declining years, declares that he wants to live. Yelena reassures
him that she, too, will soon be old. Sonya enters to announce that
Astrov has arrived in response to a summons to attend to
Serebryakov. The latter describes him as an ignoramus and refuses
to see him. He is even more distressed by the appearance of Uncle
Vanya in his dressing-gown offering to relieve Yelena's vigil. He
only softens when Marina enters and treats him like a child; he
permits her to usher him to bed. A lightning flash signals the onset

of the storm outside.

Left together on stage, Vanya complains to Yelena about his wasted life and begs her not to waste her own and to cease idle 'philosophising'. Yelena accuses him of being drunk and resists his attempt to kiss her hand. Left alone, Vanya regrets having missed the opportunity to propose to Yelena ten years previously and dreams sentimentally of what might have been. He also bewails a wasted life devoted to a miserable nonentity of a brother-in-law and feels he has been 'duped like an idiot'. Astrov enters slightly drunk and dressed in a frock-coat but minus waistcoat and tie, accompanied by Telegin. He and Vanya talk about Yelena, Astrov's drunkenness revealing a slightly cynical side to his nature. He invites Telegin to play the guitar, but when Sonya enters he excuses himself for being tie-less before exiting. Sonya complains about a state of affairs which has led to the hay lying unharvested and rotting in the rain-soaked fields, but then an expression on her face reminds Vanya of his sister, Sonya's mother, about whom he makes a few enigmatic remarks but then refuses to answer Sonya's queries.

In the following scene between Sonya and Astrov, who is now respectably dressed, the storm is beginning to abate and they decide to have a midnight feast by raiding the sideboard. Astrov complains of the bad atmosphere in the house and describes Yelena's life as one of idleness. He condemns Russian provincial life and despondently says he cares nothing for himself or for others. Sonya responds by praising his fine qualities and begs him not to destroy himself with drink. She hints at her own feelings for him in the guise of a hypothetical third person, but Astrov appears not to recognise the subterfuge while stating that he finds it impossible to love, although he is still capable of being thrilled by beauty. Left alone, Sonya laments her own plainness and is tantalised by not knowing if Astrov has any feelings for her.

The storm is now over and there follows a scene of 'sisterly' reconciliation between Sonya and her stepmother who, it seems, have not been on speaking terms. Yelena assures Sonya that she did not marry Serebryakov for money but out of admiration for his scholarship and his public position. In these moments of confessional honesty Sonya reveals her feelings for Astrov, whom Yelena goes on to portray as a man of courage, talent and freedom of mind – even if he seems a trifle coarse. She wishes

Sonya joy while seeing little happiness for herself on this earth. In making Sonya happy, Yelena has succeeded in making herself feel miserable and seeks consolation in music-making. She sends Sonya to ask permission of the professor to play the piano before calling through the open window to the watchman on his rounds, requesting that he make less noise as 'the master' is unwell. Sonya returns and tells Yelena that her husband won't allow her to play.

Act Three
The scene is the drawing-room fifteen minutes before a family council meeting which Serebryakov has called for one o'clock in the afternoon. Vanya, Sonya and Yelena have gathered before the meeting, about which Vanya is being ironic. Yelena declares she is bored and Sonya suggests she remedy this by helping with work on the estate. Sonya refers to the disturbing effect which Yelena appears to have produced on them all. She must be a witch. Vanya suggests she's a 'mermaid', then, to appease her annoyance, says he will fetch her some autumn roses. It appears that Astrov is again paying a visit and is sitting in Vanya's office painting his maps of the area. Sonya describes to Yelena her long-standing emotional attachment to Astrov and her despondency at the fact that he never appears to have noticed this. Yelena says she will ask him discreetly what his feelings for Sonya are but, in a soliloquy, she admits her own attraction to the doctor who is made to seem remarkable in an environment consisting for the most part of 'grey blobs' rather than people. She contemplates taking Vanya's previously offered advice to 'run wild' for once in her life. Yelena uses as an excuse for a meeting the fact that Astrov has expressed an interest in showing her the maps he has been making, representing three stages in the destruction of the local environment over the past fifty years, without any compensatory benefits of civilised advance. However, when it comes to the point, it is clear that Yelena is bored by Astrov's passionate ecological disquisition and seeks to turn the subject to Sonya's feelings for him. She soon elicits the information that he doesn't love Sonya. At the same time, Astrov interprets Yelena's questioning as indirect solicitation on her own behalf. He describes her as a bird of prey and a 'beautiful, silky-smooth ferret' who must have a victim. Yelena is simultaneously repelled and attracted

by this kind of talk. Astrov wishes to arrange an assignation and makes an attempt to embrace her, which Yelena half-resists, when they are interrupted by Vanya bearing the promised gift of roses. Astrov starts to make conversation about the weather, rolls up his maps, and exits. Vanya is staggered by what he has just witnessed and is then begged by Yelena to find some means of getting herself and the professor away from here, 'today!'

The family council assembles, attended by everyone apart from Astrov. Serebryakov announces that he proposes to sell the estate, invest the proceeds and buy a modest villa near St Petersburg. Vanya is flabbergasted and protests that the estate is not his to sell as it belongs to Sonya, that he personally has slaved away to pay off the mortgage as well as managing the estate for twenty-five years, regularly sending money to Serebryakov in return for an annual pittance of five hundred roubles. Serebryakov excuses himself by stressing his unworldliness in practical affairs and agreeing to the need for Sonya's consent. This does nothing to appease Vanya, who launches into a personal attack on Serebryakov, expressing contempt for his work and accusing him of being his worst enemy. Serebryakov retaliates by calling Vanya a 'nobody'. Vanya claims that, had he been able to lead a normal life, he might have been a Schopenhauer or a Dostoevsky, but realises he is talking nonsense, possibly even going mad. He exits, announcing that he'll give Serebryakov something to remember him by. Sonya, who has been silent throughout the scene having earlier gauged from Yelena what Astrov's feelings for her are, appeals distressfully to Marina like a child, before asking her father to try to understand Vanya's point of view. Yelena begs her husband to reconcile himself with Vanya. He agrees and they both exit to look for him. While Marina is attempting to comfort Sonya, a pistol shot is heard followed by a scream from Yelena. Serebryakov runs in, terrified, while Yelena is seen struggling with Vanya in the doorway in an attempt to wrest a revolver from his hand. Vanya frees himself and fires a second shot at Serebryakov, accompanying the explosion with a verbal exclamation, 'Bang!' Realising, with intense frustration, that he has missed his target for the second time he beats the floor with the revolver before sinking, exhausted, into a chair. Yelena begs to be taken away; Vanya realises the enormity of what he has just done and Sonya appeals quietly to Marina, 'Nanna! Nanna!'

Act Four

The scene is Vanya's bedroom which also doubles as the estate office and which has a section set aside for Astrov's map-making. It also has a cage with a starling and there is a map of Africa on one of the walls. It would appear to be the evening of the same day as Act Three, and Telegin and Marina are winding a skein of wool. Serebryakov and Yelena have already announced their departure for Kharkov and Marina is looking forward to the normalisation of estate life. Telegin says he's hidden the revolver in the cellar. A bottle of morphine has gone missing from Astrov's medical case, which he accuses Vanya of stealing. Vanya cannot forgive himself for having missed Serebryakov twice and wonders why nobody has come to arrest him; he decides the world must be insane and wonders how he is going to drag on to the age of sixty. Astrov descants on his favourite theme of what people of the future will think of those living in the present a couple of centuries from now, and again expresses his detestation of Russian provincial life. Sonya joins in the attempt to retrieve the morphine and urges Vanya to 'endure'. She also begs him to restore friendly relations with her father before he leaves. Vanya gives back the purloined bottle and tries to distract himself with paperwork. A scene between Astrov and Yelena follows, in which they bid farewell to each other. Astrov reminds her of the previously suggested assignation and attempts to persuade her to stay. They shake hands and Yelena steals one of his pencils as a keepsake. Astrov pronounces the end of the episode, '*Finita la commedia!*' and kisses her on the cheek while Yelena, 'just for once in my life', lets herself go and embraces him impulsively. They recoil from each other almost instantly and Astrov repeats, *Finita*!

Everyone is now on stage for the farewells and Serebryakov asks Vanya to forgive and forget, while believing he could now write a treatise on the art of living in the wake of his experiences during the past few hours. He and Vanya embrace each other three times as if nothing had happened, Vanya promising to send him a regular amount of money as before. Serebryakov's parting shot is to urge everyone to 'get down to practicalities'. The sound of harness-bells announces their departure as Vanya and Sonya seek immediate distraction in the accounts ledgers. Astrov announces that he, too, must leave, but not before accepting a glass of vodka. The vacuum left by the others' departure is felt in the desultory conversation about lame horses, blacksmiths and the heat in

Africa. Vanya makes a ledger entry as the sound of harness-bells announces Astrov's departure. Marina yawns while Telegin tunes his guitar and Sonya embarks on the speech which concludes the play, stressing that life goes on, that its trials must be endured patiently, that death will be met without complaint, and that God will pity them in the afterlife where, finally, they will find peace and rest. The speech is accompanied in its final stages by Vanya's silent tears, Telegin's strumming, the mother-in-law's marginal jotting and Marina's winding wool, before 'the curtain slowly falls'.

Commentary

Chekhov and the theatre: general background

Chekhov was active in the theatre at the height of the European Naturalist movement, the impact of which was felt both in terms of its philosophy and in its effect on staging practice. A key word in the vocabulary of the Naturalists was 'determinism'. Under the influence of those who espoused (and frequently simplified) the ideas of Charles Darwin, Karl Marx and others, human beings were seen to be psychologically, physiologically, historically, economically and environmentally subject to the 'determining' pressures of heredity and environment, or related to the lower forms of animal life. The scientific approach to reality and human affairs which this produced led, in the theatre, to the precise re-creation of ordinary, everyday environments as part of an attempt to illustrate the way in which people, either individually or in groups, were shaped by these external pressures. The democratic criteria of Naturalist ideas (democratic in so far as they embraced everybody irrespective of class and social standing) also led to an emphasis on the social norm rather than the social exception because, if everyone was subject to the same natural laws, it made little difference whether a dramatic character was of high or low estate. In fact, the Naturalist movement laid the basis for the special significance of the latter although, in actual practice, dramatists tended to concentrate on the lives of the middle classes rather than those of the 'lower orders'. In his short stories, Chekhov shows great interest in the lives of ordinary Russian people, including peasants. In his major plays, however, his interest is restricted in the main to the milieu of relatively impoverished gentrified inhabitants of superannuated country estates in the period following the emancipation of the serfs. Freedom, of sorts, was given to the Russian peasantry in 1861, the year after Chekhov was born, his important plays being written between 1887 and 1903.

Naturalism's interest in general scientific laws for human conduct tended to provide a rather reductionist perspective on life, where the 'lowest common denominator', or human average,

provided the key to any answers which were available. In dramatic
terms, this tended to produce not only a social levelling but a
flattening of distinctions between the 'dramatic' and the
'undramatic', the 'significant' and the 'insignificant', the high points
of dramatic excitement and the low points of dramatic inactivity.
It could even produce an equalisation of the comic and tragic
genres, evincing a world in which, as Chekhov said: 'People dine,
simply dine and at that moment their happiness is decided or their
lives shattered'. He also said that, 'A writer must be as objective
as a chemist . . . he must know that dung-heaps play a very
respectable part in a landscape . . .' At its most extreme, this view
could even seem to produce a world in which a death was as
significant as a yawn or where, as the doctor says in *Three Sisters*,
'*Vsyo ravno* . . .' (It's all the same . . .). In other words, there were
no significant distinctions or discriminations to be made where there
were no longer any meaningfully distinct categories or moral
certainties; no blacks or whites, but merely different shades of grey.

 Chekhov shared this dramatic landscape with some notable
contemporaries all of whom owed debts of varying degrees to the
Naturalist movement – including Ibsen, Strindberg, Hauptmann
and Shaw. It was also a period during which a previously
stagnant phase in European theatre generally was being countered
by a revival of interest in theatre as a serious art form. One
consequence was the creation of new playing spaces for the new
drama under the aegis of specialised theatre 'directors'. The
movement also inspired a new breed of actor, often amateur, but
imbued with the kind of dedication to the art of theatre which the
so-called 'professionals' seemed singularly to lack. Such were the
examples set by André Antoine and the *Théâtre Libre* in Paris,
Otto Brahm and the *Freie Bühne* in Berlin, the German Saxe-
Meiningen company who toured Europe extensively, Strindberg's
own *Intima Teatren* in Stockholm, J. T. Grein's Independent
Theatre and Granville Barker's Court Theatre in London, and
Yeats's and Lady Gregory's Abbey Theatre in Dublin. Most
influential, as far as Chekhov was concerned, and critical in
determining his world-wide renown as a dramatist, was the
creation of the Moscow Art Theatre by Stanislavsky and
Nemirovich-Danchenko, in 1897, and which between its opening,
in October 1898, and the year of Chekhov's death, in 1904,
staged all of his finest plays – *The Seagull* (1898), *Uncle
Vanya* (1899), *Three Sisters* (1901), *The Cherry Orchard*

(1904) and *Ivanov* (1904).

Naturalist drama in Russia became the almost exclusive preserve of Maxim Gorky, whose first plays, *The Merchant Class* and *The Lower Depths* (the latter set in a dosshouse), Chekhov had encouraged the Art Theatre to stage. Gorky's example had been anticipated in the work of Leo Tolstoy and others who wrote plays based on peasant life, of which the most significant was Tolstoy's own *The Power of Darkness* (1886). Chekhov, too, was aware of his debt to a Russian dramatic tradition which reached back to Gogol (in the 1830s), Turgenev (in the 1850s) and to Alexander Ostrovsky, whose dramatic output extended from *c.*1850 to *c.*1880. Chekhov's early one-act plays such as *The Bear*, *The Proposal*, *The Jubilee* and *The Wedding* appear strongly influenced by farcical and 'grotesque' elements to be found in Gogol's *The Government Inspector* and *Marriage* as well as in Turgenev's plays of the 1850s. Act Two of *Ivanov* (the soirée at the Lebedyevs') seems to combine elements of grotesquerie from both Gogol and Turgenev, as does Vanya's attempted shooting of Serebryakov in Act Three of *Uncle Vanya*. The quarrel between Lomov and his 'fiancée', in *The Proposal*, is highly reminiscent of the quarrel between brother and sister in Turgenev's *Lunch with the Marshal of the Nobility*, while Chekhov's *Wedding* would seem anticipatory of Act Three of his own *The Cherry Orchard*. In many respects, Chekhov's plays seem least like the Turgenev play with which they are frequently compared, *A Month in the Country*, which has a country estate setting in common but little else (but see p. xlv). Neither do they have much in common with the plays of Ostrovsky, although a play like *Talent and its Admirers*, with its insight into the world of the nineteenth-century acting profession, provides very useful background to an understanding of Nina's life as an actress in *The Seagull*.

Mention of this last play is a reminder of Chekhov's interest in theatrical movements other than the Naturalist. In many respects, he may be said to have shared the interest of Konstantin Treplev (in *The Seagull*) in the pursuit of 'new forms', even if he does not entirely share the young artist's spirit of hostility to Naturalist theatre in general and the way in which it reduces 'high priests in the temple of art' to ordinary mortals who 'eat and drink . . . walk about and wear their suits' in a setting which consists of 'three walls lit by artificial lighting' (trans. Frayn, 1986, p. 5). Konstantin's play-within-the-play is an early, rather inconclusive attempt to put some of the ideas of the dramatic 'Symbolists' into action. Led by the philosopher Vladimir Solovyov, who influenced the work of Andrey Bely, Alexander Blok, Leonid Andreyev and others in the early 1900s, and inspired by the work of French Symbolist poets and the work of Maurice Maeterlinck, the Russian reaction against the dominance of Naturalism in the theatre was spearheaded by members of the Russian Symbolist movement. Generally speaking, the Symbolists were reacting against the materialistic outlook enshrined in Naturalism and encouraged a resurgence of the idealistic, the aesthetic and the metaphysical. In emphasising the primary validity of 'other worlds', as an aspect of their reaction against materialism, the Symbolists tended to suggest that the one we take for granted is actually insubstantial and unreal. Towards the end of his life, Chekhov himself expressed interest in the work of Maurice Maeterlinck and encouraged the staging of work by the Belgian dramatist. Actor/directors, such as Vsevolod Meyerhold, and poet/novelists, like Andrey Bely, detected 'symbolist' elements in *The Cherry Orchard* (see Meyerhold's essay 'The Naturalistic Theatre and Theatre of Mood' in E. Braun (ed.), *Meyerhold on Theatre*, 1991, pp.23–34, and Andrey Bely's essay on *The Cherry Orchard* in L. Senelick (ed.), *Russian Dramatic Theory from Pushkin to the Symbolists*, 1981, pp.89–92) and Andrey Bely even detected quasi-symbolist elements in a play like *Ivanov* when it was staged by the Moscow Art Theatre in 1904, despite the fact that the play itself dates from the late 1880s. Just as his dramatic output straddled two centuries, Chekhov's drama also spanned a period during which major changes were taking place in the arts. To what extent his drama can then be considered to be Naturalist, Impressionist, Symbolist, Expressionist, Surrealist, or any combination of these, becomes an interesting issue in the debate surrounding the interpretation of his plays.

Playwriting was very much a second string to Chekhov's bow. His world renown as a dramatist is based on a comparatively small body of work compared with his fictional output. His current reputation as a dramatist, rather than as a writer of short stories, would undoubtedly have come as a surprise to him. Indeed, up until six years before his death, he would probably have been reconciled to his fate as a failed dramatist, given his experience of the theatre and the attempts made to stage his plays during his lifetime. The one-act 'jokes', which he claimed to have written in hours rather than days, were produced just as successfully, if not more so, as the full-length plays which cost him so much time and effort, although the influence of the former on the latter should not be underestimated.

Staging of Chekhov's plays during his lifetime

The first production of *Ivanov*, at the Korsh Theatre, Moscow, in 1887 was under-rehearsed and something of a shambles, as Chekhov's letter to his brother testifies (see Simon Karlinsky and Michael Heim, *Letters of Anton Chekhov*, London, Bodley Head, 1973, pp.72–3). The revised version was subsequently staged in St Petersburg with greater success, but the première of *The Wood Demon*, at the Abramova Theatre, Moscow, in 1889 was as discouraging as the première of *Ivanov* had been. The first performance of *The Seagull* in 1896, which Chekhov attended in St Petersburg, was not so disastrous a production as history has suggested, largely because the director, Yevtikhi Karpov, was a highly competent producer and Vera Komissarzhevskaia, who played Nina, a very fine actress. The première was a flop largely because the audience had expected it to be a benefit performance for one of the theatre's leading ladies and had arrived anticipating the typical comedy with which her reputation had been made. Not surprisingly, they were bitterly disappointed by the non-appearance of their favourite and totally bemused by the play, which called itself a 'comedy' and ended with a suicide.

Chekhov's dramatic rehabilitation was directly attributable to the enthusiastic propagandising of his merits by Vladimir Nemirovich-Danchenko, who was himself a dramatist and closely associated with the Maly Theatre, as well as being a teacher of drama and theatre studies at the Moscow Philharmonic School. When deciding, together with Stanislavsky, on the repertoire for the Moscow Art Theatre's first season, it was Nemirovich who advocated reviving *The Seagull* in the face of his partner's general coolness towards the modern repertoire and ignorance of Chekhov's work. Chekhov needed some persuading in the wake of the 1896 débâcle but, reluctantly, agreed without any great hopes of success, given an untried company in untried circumstances. The rest is history. Stanislavsky prepared a detailed production score for the play (itself a very unusual procedure at the time – see S. D. Balukhaty (ed.), '*The Seagull' Produced by Stanislavsky*, 1952); the play then went into extended rehearsal and opened to great public acclaim in December 1898. Critics were rather less enthusiastic than the general public, however, and tended to dislike what they saw as the play's pessimism and the excessively naturalistic elements in its production. Chekhov was himself critical of the production when he was given a private performance, without décor, in 1899. He was especially critical of Stanislavsky's interpretation of Trigorin as a rather wan and spineless aesthete, as well as the interpretation of Nina as someone permanently overwrought.

He was more pleased with the production of *Uncle Vanya*, which followed (see pp.li–liv). From this point on, Chekhov drew ever closer to the Art Theatre, largely on account of his attachment to the Theatre's leading lady, Olga Knipper. His last two plays were written especially for the Moscow Art Theatre and with specific members of the company in mind.

Three Sisters was given its première in January 1901 and, although not an instant success, confirmed Chekhov's status as a major dramatist. (For an account of the production based on Stanislavsky's score, see R. Russell and A. Barratt (eds), *Russian Theatre in the Age of Modernism*, 1990.) Despite its description as a 'drama' on the play's title page, Chekhov insisted he had written 'a comedy'. Disputes about the generic nature of the work accompanied it at the time and have continued to do so ever since. Chekhov attended rehearsals and was particularly anxious about the accuracy of 'effects', such as that of the fire in Act Three. He also submitted to demands that the ending of the play be rewritten. In the original version, the body of the dead Baron was to be carried on stage but, fearing that the cramped conditions at the 'Ermitazh' theatre would not permit this without rocking the scenery, Stanislavsky asked that the scene be omitted. He also felt that the presence of the corpse rendered the play's ending too morbid – a point with which Chekhov concurred.

By the time the Moscow Art Theatre came to stage *The Cherry Orchard* in 1904, it had moved from the Ermitazh on Carriage Row to newly converted premises near the city centre (where it remains housed to this day). Chekhov was already terminally ill and the length of time he took to compose the play was due to

the intense physical difficulties he was experiencing, quite apart
from the intrinsic problems of writing the play. In the
circumstances, it is amazing that what emerged was described by
Chekhov as 'a comedy . . . even, in places, a farce'. Needless to
say, Stanislavsky insisted that Chekhov did not understand what he
had written and that the play was, by any normal standards, 'a
tragedy'. He had been moved to tears while reading it. Despite
Chekhov's protests, Stanislavsky began work on the production
score firmly convinced that he was right and that the author was
wrong. However, the actual score that emerged would seem to
have been more faithful to Chekhov's intentions than has, hitherto,
been assumed (see 'Stanislavsky's Production Score for Chekhov's
The Cherry Orchard (1904): A Synoptic Overview' in *Modern
Drama*, Vol. xlii, No. 4, Winter 1999, pp.519–40).

   Despite his illness, Chekhov insisted on attending rehearsals. He
sat at the back of the auditorium, refusing invitations to sit in the
director's chair. He offered suggestions and comments, particularly
on how best to achieve certain effects like the famous sound of the
'breaking string', all of which went unheeded. Eventually, he
became disillusioned and stopped attending. Not only were his
suggestions being ignored but almost every proposal he made with
regard to casting was disregarded. He was especially anxious about
the casting of Charlotta, whom he thought Knipper should have
played. Knipper was less than suitably cast as Ranyevskaya and
Charlotta's role was given to an actress whom Chekhov considered
to lack a sense of humour. Chekhov had cast Stanislavsky as
Lopakhin while composing the play, with the result that the
Theatre chose Leonidov for the part. Stanislavsky played Gayev.
And so on . . . Chekhov was both irritated by this and dismayed
by reports he received during rehearsals, which seemed to give
misleading accounts of the play's action. He concluded, after the
première, that Stanislavsky had 'ruined' his play. Matters were not
helped by his having been asked to cut the ending to Act Two and
include some of its elements at the beginning of the act. When
Chekhov died in July, approximately five months after the play's
opening, he must have thought he would go down in history as a
dramatist destined for the lower divisions of theatre history.
However, to adapt Olga's final line in *Three Sisters*: If only he
knew. If only he knew . . . !

From *Wood Demon* to *Vanya*

The Wood Demon began life as a joint project between Chekhov and his friend, the journalist, playwright and publisher, Aleksei Suvorin, and was written in the wake of *Platonov* (a play which remained undiscovered until 1920), and *Ivanov* (1887). In a letter to Suvorin, dated 18 October 1888, Chekhov sketched outlines of the characters, some of whom re-emerged in recognisable form in *Uncle Vanya* and, as such, they may be considered relevant to an understanding of the later play. Serebryakov was originally called Blagosvetlov, of whom Chekhov wrote:

> From the moment he first opens his mouth he produces an exhausting and irritating impression [...] Blagosvetlov must impress the audience both as an intelligent, gout-ridden old codger and as a boring piece of music which has been played too long. [...] Blagosvetlov [is a] member of the Council of State, who has received the Order of the White Eagle and has a pension of 7,200 roubles. Comes from a priest's family, and was educated at a church school. Attained his position by his own efforts. His past is without blemish. Suffers from gout, rheumatism, insomnia and a noise in his ears. Has received some landed property as part of his wife's dowry. Is definitely intelligent. Cannot stand mystics, visionaries, crackpots, lyric poets, prigs, doesn't believe in God and is accustomed to judge everything in this world from the point of view of deeds. Deeds, deeds, deeds. And all the rest is nonsense or charlatanism. [...] I want Blagosvetlov to feel himself surrounded by crackpots. (*The Wood Demon, Uncle Vanya*, trans. Hingley, 1964, pp.273–7)

The original Sonya was called Nastya and, according to Chekhov,

> is twenty-three or twenty-four years old. Is well educated and can think for herself. [...] Has never been in love. Lazy, likes abstract discussions, reads books lying down. Wants to get married only for the sake of variety and so as not to be left on the shelf. Says she can only love somebody interesting. [...] Having seen and heard the Wood-Demon [i.e. Khrushchev, the prototype of Astrov], she gives way to passion to the ultimate degree [...] Nastya likes him, not because of his ideas, which are foreign to her, but because of his gifts, his passion and the wide range of his thought. She likes the fact that his brain has gone striding through the whole of Russia and landed up ten centuries ahead of us. (Ibid., pp.274–5)

The original Astrov was at this stage called Korovin and described as

> a landowner of between thirty and thirty-three years of age, the
> Wood-Demon. A poet and landscape painter with a tremendous
> feeling for nature. Once while he was still at high school he planted
> a silver birch in his yard. When it became green and began to sway
> in the breeze and to rustle and cast a small shadow, his heart filled
> with pride. He'd helped God to create a new birch-tree, made the
> world richer by one tree! This was the beginning of his peculiar
> form of creativity. He brings his idea to fruition not on canvas or
> paper, but in the ground, not in terms of dead paint, but in terms
> of organisms. A tree is a beautiful thing, but it also has the right to
> life, it is as necessary as water, sunlight and stars. Life on this earth
> is unthinkable without trees. Forests condition climate, climate
> influences people's character, etc. etc. There can be neither
> civilization nor happiness if the forests go crashing down beneath
> the axe, if the climate is cruel and rough and if people are cruel
> and rough as well. The future is horrible. (Ibid., p.275)

The original Vanya was named Vasili Volkov but his biographical
details are very much like those of the later Vanya. He is
described as [the]

> brother of Blagosvetlov's deceased wife. Manages Blagosvetlov's
> estate (he has got through his own some time previously). Regrets
> never having stolen anything. Did not expect his relatives from St
> Petersburg to show so little appreciation of his efforts. They don't
> understand him and don't want to understand him [...] Drinks
> Vichy water and grumbles. (Ibid., p.276)

A comparison of the projected *dramatis personae* with those of
The Wood Demon and *Uncle Vanya* is instructive:

Draft sketches	The Wood Demon	Uncle Vanya
Blagosvetlov	Serebryakov	Serebryakov
–	Yelena	Yelena
Boris (his son)	–	–
Nastya	Sonya	Sonya
Anuchin (a landowner)	Ivan Orlovski	–
–	Fedor Orlovski (his son)	–

Korovin (the Wood Demon)	Khrushchev	Astrov
Galakhov (a wealthy civil servant)	Zheltukhin	–
Liuba (his sister)	Yulia	–
Volkov	Georges	Vanya
–	Diadin	Telegin
–	Vassili (Zheltukhin's manservant)	–
Semyon (a labourer)	Semyon	–
–	Maria Vasilyevna	Maria Vasilyevna
Mlle Emilie (elderly Frenchwoman)	–	–
Feodosy (a wandering pilgrim)	–	–
–	–	Marina
–	Watchman	Watchman
–	–	Worker

Laurence Senelick provides a useful insight into Chekhov's working methods in itemising the attributes which some of the characters of *The Wood Demon* share with those of the later play:

> Khrushchyov's priggishness was diluted by Fyodor's dissipation to form the idealistic but hard-drinking Astrov; Voynitsky's [Georges] glumness was crossed with Zheltukhin's fussy wooing to compose Vanya. Sofiya [Sonya] the bluestocking and Yuliya the compulsive housekeeper were merged in Sonya. Yelena became less altruistic; and, most significantly, the role of Marina the nanny was added, to provide another, more objective viewpoint. (Senelick, 1985, p.91)

In the introduction to his recent translation of *Uncle Vanya*, Stephen Mulrine describes some of the main similarities, differences and transpositions between the two plays:

> All the plot ingredients of *Uncle Vanya* are present in *The Wood Demon*: the conflict between Serebryakov and Vanya; the latter's infatuation with the Professor's young wife; Sonya's troubled love for the environmentalist doctor; Yelena's coy interest in him. Much of the incident is also common to both plays: the doctor and Vanya engage in a dispute about forest conservation; Vanya makes a clumsy pass at Yelena; someone walks in on an apparent embrace; Serebryakov outlines his scheme to sell off the estate; Vanya exits in

a rage, and an off-stage pistol shot is heard. In fact, almost the entire content of Acts II and III of *Uncle Vanya* is recycled from *The Wood Demon*. The difference is that the sequence of events is now purposefully connected, and the obscuring detail cut away. In *The Wood Demon*, for example, it is the doctor, Khrushchev, and not Uncle Georges, who chances upon what he interprets as a lovers' tryst, but which is quite innocent, certainly on Yelena's part. However, Uncle Georges' suicidal depression, which culminates in the fatal pistol shot, is later revealed to have been partly fuelled by the slanderous rumours circulating about his relationship with the Professor's wife. That revelation is made in Act IV of *The Wood Demon*, through a narrated account of the discovery of Uncle Georges' diary, and Chekhov would never again employ so transparently unconvincing a device. Given that Act III closes on a genuinely tragic note, the picnic atmosphere of Act IV is also discordant [...] Among the more important changes, the 'reversal' of the interrupted embrace, in which it is now Vanya, clutching his peace-offering of autumn roses, who walks in on Astrov, is at once both comical, and inexpressibly poignant. The genius of the mature Chekhov is shown again in the scene of the off-stage pistol shot. Given Vanya's state of mind, we have every reason to expect suicide, so that when he re-enters in pursuit of Serebryakov, the shock is palpable. (*Uncle Vanya*, trans. and intro. Stephen Mulrine, London, Nick Hern Books, 1999, pp.xvii–xix)

Of especial note is the overall reduction in the number of characters in *Uncle Vanya*, which is also Chekhov's shortest full-length play and considerably shorter than *The Wood Demon*. The later work also abandons the rather old-fashioned division of each act into separate 'scenes', which characterised the writing not only of *The Wood Demon* but also *Platonov* and *Ivanov*. This makes the structural composition of the play more like *The Seagull* and would therefore seem to indicate that *Uncle Vanya* was completed during the mid- rather than the early-1890s, although evidence exists to support both conjectural dates. Maurice Valency, unjustly, called *The Wood Demon* 'a piece of theatrical rubbish' compared to *Uncle Vanya*, which he described as 'one of the great plays of our time' (Valency, 1966, p.180).

A curious feature of the later play is the decision to name it after Vanya rather than the 'wood demon' figure, Astrov, especially since, unlike Vanya, Georges commits suicide in the earlier play – a fact which renders him, dramatically, more of a

prominent figure than Vanya, who not only does not attempt
suicide, but fails to commit murder twice. However, Astrov is no
more of a central figure in the later play than Khrushchev had
been in *The Wood Demon* so there is even a puzzle over the
naming of the earlier play. Both doctors are given ecological
enthusiasms and they even engage in the same pastimes of map-
drawing – Khrushchev in Act Four of his play, Astrov in Act
Three of his, but otherwise they have little in common. Moreover,
if one compares Chekhov's description of Korovin with his later
manifestations as Khrushchev and Astrov, there seems a strikingly
ironical mismatch between the rather idealised conception of the
prototype and the eventual characters themselves.

Where *Uncle Vanya* is characterised by unity of place (all three
acts take place on the Serebryakov estate) only Acts Two and
Three of *The Wood Demon* are similarly set, the first taking place
on the neighbouring Zheltukhin estate and the fourth at a watermill which Diadin (the Telegin figure) has hired from Khrushchev.
However, although the Act One locations are different, Chekhov
transfers chunks of dialogue, virtually intact, from the earlier play
to the later. For example, much of the material on pp. 6–7 is
taken unabridged from *The Wood Demon* and the same is true of
pp.11–12, while Astrov's speech beginning 'You can burn peat in
your stoves . . .' (p.11) is virtually identical with one by
Khrushchev in *The Wood Demon*. Even some of the more trivial
detail finds its way from the earlier play into the later, such as
Astrov's reference to his moustache on p.4, which repeats an
observation which Zheltukhin had made about his own facial hair.
Similarly, remarks about the samovar having lost its heat (p.8)
echo those about a pie having cooled in *The Wood Demon*. On
p.11, Sonya's speech in praise of conservation is a repetition of a
similar speech made by Georges in *The Wood Demon*, the
difference being the un-ironical nature of her version, while the
scene between Vanya and Yelena at the end of the first act
replicates one in *The Wood Demon* apart from the fact that, in
the former, a game of croquet is taking place in the background.

Act Two of *Uncle Vanya* repeats much of Act Two of *The
Wood Demon* although Fedor Orlovski assumes Astrov's role on
p.21, where he enters 'wrapped in a blanket' rather than wearing a
frock coat and, on p.22, it is he who makes a rapid exit while
excusing himself for not wearing a tie, which is even more
incongruous in the circumstances than Astrov's similar exit in

Uncle Vanya. Fedor is also given Astrov's taste for vodka and a lecherous interest in Yelena, which Khrushchev does not share in the earlier play. Instead, Khrushchev is more of a stern moraliser convinced that Yelena is a faithless female who is having an affair with Georges, whereas in fact the latter's overtures, like Vanya's, are repulsed. There are important differences in the night-time scene between Sonya and the doctor. In the earlier play Khrushchev declares his love for her (unlike Astrov in *Uncle Vanya*) but similarly announces that love is not the basis of his entire being. Sonya is embarrassed by his declaration that he wants to take her away from 'the poisoned atmosphere' of the house (a phrase which Astrov also uses). The act concludes in the same manner in both versions.

Act Three of *Uncle Vanya* is more or less identical with *The Wood Demon* from the beginning of the family council scene to the end of the act, apart from Khrushchev's intervention in the council scene of the earlier play to protest against the professor's apparent intention to sell off the estate timber. Astrov's request to Yelena to grant him an assignation is given to Fedor Orlovski in *The Wood Demon*, where it is answered by a slap in the face. The most crucial difference consists in the conclusion to Act Three of *The Wood Demon* with Georges's suicide, as opposed to Vanya's attempted murder of Serebryakov in *Uncle Vanya*.

The fourth act of *Uncle Vanya* has little in common with *The Wood Demon*. Astrov's ecological disquisition to Yelena over his maps in Act Three takes place in Act Four of the earlier play, but in a much shorter scene and with Sonya rather than Yelena on the receiving end. Serebryakov's lines about having acquired enough experience to write a treatise on the art of living, and his injunction to 'get down to practicalities', are among the few lines carried over from Act Four of *The Wood Demon* into the later play.

Comparing *The Wood Demon* with *Uncle Vanya*, critics have seen the spirit of the former as belonging to a 'Tolstoyan' phase in Chekhov's artistic development, influenced by the philosophical views of the great nineteenth-century Russian writer Count Leo Tolstoy (1828–1910). This implies a belief in the possibility of people's moral conversion and reconciliation with each other and with their common human plight through a quasi-religious sense of unity, both with the world of nature and with that of a simple, uncorrupted peasantry. The play certainly describes a tangle of

complicated and unpleasant human relations among educated
people against the backdrop of a serenely indifferent natural world.
Moreover, the conclusion appears to provide an optimistic
resolution to the personal conflicts as couples are either paired off
or harmoniously reconciled with each other. However, this
interpretation needs to be seen against the fact of Georges's suicide
in Act Three, and the other characters' apparent indifference to it,
which colours the play's final moments – quite apart from the fact
that the joyous pairing of the ecologist Khrushchev with Sonya
takes place, ironically, against the background of a forest fire
blazing in the distance.

By contrast, in *Uncle Vanya*, the moral perspective appears to be
more neutral and the intellectual irony more intense. The rather
diffuse and varied action of *The Wood Demon* has become more
condensed, more monochrome, and has acquired a unity of mood
and feeling which almost belies the play's division into four
separate acts. The backdrop of the natural world is less obtrusive
and the human isolation of the characters is felt all the more
powerfully as a result. The pattern of arrival and departure,
characteristic of *The Seagull*, *Three Sisters* and *The Cherry
Orchard*, is also a feature of *Uncle Vanya* where the arrival of
outsiders causes turmoil in the settled lives of country-estate
inhabitants. In some ways, the play can be seen as a unique fusion
of nineteenth-century naturalistic observation and twentieth-century
absurdist sentiment.

Uncle Vanya and Nanna Marina

The title of Chekhov's fourth full-length play (*Diadia Vania* in
Russian) has often struck critics as curious. Why rework a play
originally entitled *Leshii* (*The Wood Demon*) and retitle it *Uncle
Vanya* when the nature of the protagonist's familial relationship
appears to be of little significance? He is 'uncle' to no one but
Sonya, the only person who refers to him as such apart from
Astrov, who does so ironically. Vanya is the diminutive of 'Ivan',
or 'John' in English, so that a similar English play might be
called *Uncle Johnny* or *Uncle Jacky,* the familiar form of the name
tending to place it within a family context determined by the
adult's relationship with the children. The Russian word for 'uncle'
(*diadia*) also has a colloquial use and can be used to refer to

someone familiarly, and slightly comically, as an 'old boy' or a
'bloke'. To find an approximate phonetic English equivalent of the
Russian title, one would need to resort to the linguistic realm of
children's literature or the nursery – something like *Uncle Bunkle*.
Mark Rozovski, a dramatist and theatre director who staged a
production of *Uncle Vanya* in 1993, has this to say about the
play's title:

> The title is simple, boring, does not sound very theatrical, in a
> word, not good box-office. Uncle, aunt, daddy, mummy – none of
> this strikes a chord, appeals to the ear or has drawing power. Every
> 'uncle' sounds slightly comic. The word often produces a smile, its
> sound constructed on the repetition of two strange combinations of
> the 'dia' sound, in itself somewhat parodical, more redolent of
> baby-talk such as 'dia-dia' – a sort of literal 'dadaism'. And here as
> well is the flattened sound of 'Vania'. What an original Russian
> name! Moreover – there are eight letters, made up of three 'ia's
> and two 'd's. Eight letters consisting of two four-letter words, the
> equivalence of their sequencing giving the title a hidden rhythm,
> which together with the sound weaves a spell and casts a charm.
> (M.G. Rozovskii, 'Chitaem *Diadiu Vaniu* (Deistvie pervoe)', in
> V.Ya. Lakshin et al. (eds), *Chekhoviana: Melikhovskie trudy i dni*,
> Moscow, Nauka, 1995, p.169)

This seems very relevant to an appreciation of the play's mood
and subject matter. However, while Rozovski notes the triple
repetition of the 'ia', he does not draw attention to the syllable's
semantic meaning, 'Ia' (or 'Ya') also being the first person singular
in Russian, the equivalent of 'I' in English. In this respect, it is
notable how the characters in Chekhov seem obsessed with
themselves to the exclusion of others and of society as a whole.
This was certainly true of the heroes of his earlier plays, where
both Platonov and Ivanov appear self-obsessed to the point of
caricature, so that the almost incidental, even farcical, nature of
their deaths emerges as a seemingly appropriate comment on the
grotesquely inflated consequence which they have attributed to
their individual selves. It is also the case in Chekhov's plays that
characters appear fixated on childhood or display symptoms of
arrested emotional development.

In *Uncle Vanya*, the characters' emotional immaturity manifests
itself in almost every instance, whether one thinks of Yelena's,

probably asexual, reasons for marrying Serebryakov; the latter's, at times, childlike dependence on others; the manner of Vanya's adolescent wooing of Yelena; Sonya's naive, schoolgirl infatuation with Astrov; or Astrov's own childhood reminiscences and his immersion in pursuits of the primary school (colouring maps). The characters in *Uncle Vanya* appear preoccupied with themselves and with the satisfaction of personal needs to the exclusion of everything else. Like a child, the repeated syllables of the play's title appear to shriek '*Ia! Ia! Ia!*' ('Me! me! me!') in a way which extends beyond Vanya himself to embrace just about everyone else in the play.

It might also be said that the characters' cause for complaint is not very great since this particular group of grown-ups consists of well-fed individuals who are socially and intellectually privileged. Their desires are of a contradictory nature and seem both to demand and, at the same time, to resist satisfaction. Their mode of existence could be characterised as the persistent cries of the eternally plaintive, which, were they to *be* answered would seemingly negate the very grounds of their being. By these lights, Sonya's soulful litany at the end of the play could be seen to emerge less as a result of the thwarting of her love for Astrov or as expression of any other general discontent, than as a natural emanation from an almost nun-like personality – the possibility of her ever having found happiness in marriage to Astrov seems positively hopeless in the circumstances. Similarly, Vanya's pursuit of Yelena seems to go through the mere motions of love, both demanding recognition and, simultaneously, begging to be spurned. Yelena, likewise, wishes both for her physical beauty to be appreciated through its power to attract, and for her moral rectitude to be valued through its power to repel. Finally, Astrov's apparent desire to seduce her seems both purposefully pursued and, for most of its duration, indecisively negotiated, as if success might compromise the solitary bachelor status to which he clings, as he does to his condition of unreconstructed alcoholic and disgruntled medical practitioner.

The idea of childhood and childlike behaviour being prolonged into adulthood can be found in Chekhov's other late plays, such as *Three Sisters* and *The Cherry Orchard*, but the question of their thematic origins in *Uncle Vanya* can possibly be traced to *The Wood Demon*. The first act of the earlier play takes place on

Zheltukhin's birthday in the presence of a character, Orlovski, who
has been godfather to two of the female characters. The emphasis
on birth and baptism, which associates the adults with a state of
being newly-born is contained both in the repetition of the word
'novorozhdennyi' (newly-born) and in the conventional Russian
birthday greeting, 'S novorozhdennym!', which literally means
'Happy new birth!'.

When it came to revising the work as Uncle Vanya, the idea of
being an infant again, but without the sense of moral and spiritual
rebirth, might have been at the back of Chekhov's mind. The most
significant example of this becomes the moment in Act Three when
the adult Vanya fires real bullets at Serebryakov but, like a child
at play, shouts 'Bang!'. It is interesting to note in the Russian
original that when Vanya makes his stage entry in Act One, like
an infant that has just been woken from a post-feed nap, the first
words he utters are 'Da . . . (Pause.) Da . . .'.

But what is Nanna Marina doing in the play? Every other
character in Uncle Vanya has a predecessor in The Wood Demon
apart from Marina, so why did Chekhov introduce her? This
rather ordinary, maternal figure has been accorded various kinds of
symbolic significance. She has been described as a 'Mother Russia'
figure, while her knitting has been interpreted as that of a
revolutionary tricoteuse at the foot of the guillotine; or a mock-
Penelope from The Odyssey unravelling at night what she has
knitted during the day; or as Clotho, one of the three Greek
figures of Fate associated with spinning. This desire to attribute
rather grandiose significance to Marina goes hand-in-hand with a
tendency to romanticise the other characters in the play, so that
Yelena is identified as a Helen of Troy figure (she is described as
such in The Wood Demon); Astrov is idealistically linked with the
stars (from the Latin astrum, meaning 'a star'); Vanya is described
as having warrior-like instincts because his surname contains the
Russian word for 'warrior' (voin); Serebryakov's name becomes
associated with value (serebro, meaning 'silver'); and Maria
Vasilyevna is identified with the world of philosophy and/or
politics through her pamphlets. Telegin, on the other hand, seems
impossible to idealise as his name comes from the Russian for a
'cart' (telega). 'Marina', however, derives from the Latin marinus
('pertaining to the sea') but Marina's connection with the sea is
about as remote as Yelena's connection with the mermaid (rusalka;

p.32), or Astrov's with astronomy (p.17). The play sets its face firmly against any kind of romantic aggrandisement, or even heightened significance, which is why Vanya's self-comparison with Schopenhauer and Dostoevsky seems so absurd. Chekhov appears to go out of his way to insist on the ordinary, everyday banality of this kind of life.

If Marina herself has no connection with the sea, nevertheless her name has connotations found in many European languages which link the sea with motherhood, or the origin of life (*mare/madre*; *mer/mère*;). However, once again, these associations are without any kind of mythical resonance or significance. Nor is she 'Mother Earth', or even, as Siegfried Melchinger suggests, 'Mother Russia' (*Anton Chekhov*, New York, F. Ungar, 1972, p.116), but simply a maternal figure around whom everything else meaninglessly and repetitively revolves. The physical and spiritual nourishment with which she supplies her 'children' are of an extremely mundane, even primitive, order – the ritual of tea-drinking and a stubbornly unquestioning faith in God's providence. Her presence is a symbolic one almost despite herself, whether expressing concern for her (metaphorically human) chicks which might become prey to crows, or winding wool for the endless knitting of stockings. Her peasant ordinariness and physical and mental stability (Chekhov stresses her physical immobility at the outset) are clearly aspects which others depend on in their own unstable worlds, while her comparative silence, punctuated by clichés and homilies, is in direct contrast to the volubility of the protagonists, which she describes as mere 'cackle'.

In an important sense, Marina may be said to occupy the play's centre and to preside over its action. However, she embodies this role vacuously, as if occupying a centre of absent meaning, while her main creative activity can be seen to function as a metaphor for the play itself. Her endless knitting also has a beginning, a middle and an end, commencing as a skein a wool, which is then wound into a ball, which is then knitted into a stocking. There seems to be absolutely nothing in the play which is invested with greater significance than this most humdrum of domestic activities which, in its turn, finds intellectual and emotional equivalence in talk that is a kind of endless verbal 'knitting', in the grandmother's repeated (and, we imagine, pointless) marginal jottings, and in Telegin's persistent guitar-strumming.

Time and character/duration and endurance

Uncle Vanya is a play in which the characters are very conscious
of time and of suffering. It is as if the fact of having to spend time
living a life involves having to endure an inevitable burden of
suffering. Critics who have noted this aspect of the play have
tended, more recently, to link Chekhov with the world of Samuel
Beckett and the latter's notion of 'the suffering of being' (see
below, p.xlvii). The play is certainly very aware of time – the
eleven years, approximately, which have passed since Astrov visited
the estate during the lifetime of the professor's deceased first wife;
the six years during which Sonya has kept her love of Astrov a
secret; the ten years since Vanya missed an opportunity to propose
to Yelena; the hundreds of years of life on the planet which affect
human beings and the natural world, about which Astrov
speculates; the thousand years from now when human beings will
eventually be happy; the ten years in which Astrov says he has
'become a different man' (p.3), as well as the sense that he has
had his day (aged about thirty-seven); the month he says he has
spent neglecting his responsibilities; the five or six years Yelena
declares it will take her to become 'old' (p.17); the number of
years Vanya says he may be forced to endure between his present
age (forty-seven) and sixty; the ten years in which Astrov declares
'this narrow provincial life [has] poisoned our blood' (p.51); the
twenty-five years which Vanya says he has spent wasting a life
devoted to the professor; the hundred years he, jokingly, says the
professor intends to live with them; the possible thousand-year
lifespan of a newly planted sapling.

  The play is also very precise about days, hours and minutes. It
opens during the early afternoon and Marina complains, during
the course of the act, about the disruption caused by the arrival of
the professor – where dinner used to be at one p.m. it is now
demanded at seven in the evening, followed by tea at two o'clock
in the morning; moreover, the samovar has been on the table for
'two hours' (p.5). It was the third week in Lent when the shunter
died on the operating table; it is twenty past twelve at the
beginning of Act Two; a quarter to one at the beginning of Act
Three; Sonya refers to being at church 'last Sunday' (p.26). There
is Serebryakov's sense of his declining years and being too old for
a young wife, as well as the 'few short hours' (p.55) through
which he says he has undergone so much that he could write a
treatise on the art of living. There is reference to the one occasion

per month that Astrov allows himself the pleasure of map-drawing, as well as the fifty years of ecological change represented by the maps themselves. Finally, the last scene includes the dates of invoices, 2 and 16 February, alongside references to the long succession of days and endless evenings which Sonya says they will have to live through before death.

Almost everyone in the play is aware of the consequences of passing time and the process of ageing and they constantly descant on this theme. On the other hand, there *is* the occasional moment of joy, such as Sonya's at the end of Act Two, but it seems to be gained at the expense of Yelena's simultaneous expression of unhappiness. Nobody in the play is happy, with the possible exception of the watchman who is heard singing during Act Two, but at the end of the act he is told to be quiet. In this context, just as Marina's concern is to protect her chicks from marauding crows so the watchman's function can be seen as the symbolic equivalent of protecting the estate's inhabitants from the predations of Life itself.

In the gap between the cradle and grave the characters look back nostalgically to childhood, talk about themselves and their feelings ('To have lived is not enough for them. / They have to talk about it', Samuel Beckett, *Waiting for Godot,* 2nd ed., London, Faber & Faber, 1965, p.63), either complain about or avoid work, bicker, thwart each other, and express the wish to live more fully while actually fearing anything remotely like full-blooded experience. They feel old before their time and hanker after the peace and security of oblivion. At the same time, it has to be admitted that these are real people who feel trapped by circumstances in situations from which they long to escape and about which they feel a justified sense of bitterness and frustration.

Chekov's viewpoint might be said to be similar to someone like Bernard Shaw, who saw the true joy of life in 'being used for a purpose recognised by yourself as a mighty one; the being thoroughly worn out before you are thrown on the scrap heap; the being a force of Nature instead of a feverish selfish little clod of ailments and grievances complaining that the world will not devote itself to making you happy' (Epistle Dedicatory to *Man and Superman*, Harmondsworth, Penguin Books, 1946, p.32). At the time of writing *Uncle Vanya* Chekhov had been suffering from tuberculosis for a number of years but, despite this, uncomplainingly devoted himself to his patients and to educational projects. He also undertook a punishing journey across Russia to Sakhalin Island and published a book-length sociological report on his findings while simultaneously producing some of the greatest fiction and drama of the age. In these circumstances, could he be expected to feel anything less than impatience with this totally unproductive group of irresponsible people? Although he recognised that their self-destructive solipsism represented exemplary dramatic material he seems also to have been capable of feeling sympathy for characters whose plight, if inestimable in the scale of things, can appear both pathetic and moving. At the same time he ensures that our empathy does not exclude the possibility of laughter.

Critics tends to identify Serebryakov as the villain of the piece, but he might genuinely be said to have something to complain about. Crotchety and demanding, the target of everyone else's complaints, he does however appear to have achieved distinction and public recognition; we do not have to take Vanya's estimation of his supposed intellectual nullity. He is old, no longer on a professor's salary, deprived of the world he enjoyed belonging to, and suffers from the ailments which accompany old age. He actually behaves quite reasonably when he encounters opposition, does not hand Vanya over to the police, and decides to leave for perfectly understandable reasons.

Astrov is a doctor with a constituency of impoverished peasants but seems only too willing to answer the summons of someone he views as an irritable hypochondriac so as to be in the presence of the latter's beautiful young wife. As a conservationist he appears to prefer passively to record ecological devastation rather than actively engage in practical measures to prevent it. He also blames the peasants for the process of destruction rather than 'civilizing factors' (p.36) in the form of industrialisation, which he seems to welcome. He enjoys making speeches which contrive to be self-approving even when self-denigrating and, although not quite the 'holy fool' (p.17) described by Serebryakov, he does seem to be characterised by a kind of self-conscious eccentricity. To be aware, and able to speak of, his own failings seems a tactic to exonerate himself from personal responsibility. Even the death of the shunter under chloroform, which he refers to first in the presence of Marina (p.4) and secondly Sonya (p.26), seems a plea for sympathy for his own plight rather than a recognition of the suffering of others. On the other hand, it could be argued that the play shows Astrov responding to extraordinary circumstances and that, under normal conditions, he is a responsible practitioner who attends his patients on a regular basis and only pays monthly visits to the estate.

And what about Vanya himself? Here is someone who seems to have devoted himself quite happily for twenty-five years, less to the fulfilment of his own life, than to looking after the affairs of another. Why has he done this and why, all of a sudden, does he seem to have had a change of heart? One can reasonably speculate that his sense of devotion to the professor was actually based on a sense of devotion to his dead sister and to Sonya. It has continued beyond the former's death but has then ceased when the professor chose to replace the dead sister with a similarly youthful alternative. It could be argued that Vanya sees this as an act of betrayal, which in a psychologically complicated way he seeks to avenge by wooing the new wife away from her husband – an action which is simultaneously a Freudian wooing of a simulacrum of his own sister. It might, however, be argued that Vanya's hostility towards the professor is based in feelings of poor self-esteem and genuine disillusion with Serebryakov's achievements in life, which Vanya no longer thinks worthy of his efforts. Was he happy to support Serebryakov when he considered the professor was producing valuable work but has since become dissatisfied on discovering that someone he admired has proved to have feet of clay? Or perhaps it is merely his jealousy of the professor for carrying off the very woman he himself might have wooed that leads him to denigrate the professor's academic achievement.

And what about poor Sonya? Although she is described as an orphan (p.46), her father is of course alive, if apparently uncaring. It is not clear how close Sonya was to her mother or what age she was when the latter died. When reference is made by Vanya, rather ambiguously, to his sister's suffering (p.23, also referred to by Marina on p.18), Sonya appears not to understand what is meant by this, as if she was either too young at the time or does not recognise whatever it is that is being referred to. Since her mother's death, her father would seem to have abandoned her to the tender mercies of a surrogate parent, in the form of her uncle, whom she has helped in the running of the estate. In this latter connection, Sonya appears to have been curiously ineffective, leaving any dealings with the peasants in the hands of Marina and neglecting the hay harvest. She has also nursed an unrequited love for Astrov, who is revealed during the course of the play to be a not altogether appropriate object for her affections, despite her tendency to idealise him. It is she who articulates the need to 'endure' rather than 'live' a life which seems a burdensome obligation. Her famous final speech takes the form of an escapist vision which suggests that, vocationally, she should have been a nun, immured in a cell far away from an unhappy world of complicated relationships, and contemplating a life after death as a palliative for the one she should have been trying to live more fully in this world. How this final scene is performed becomes crucial to an overall interpretation of the play. Are we being invited to weep buckets of empathy, 'watching the end through a mist of tears', as the *Guardian* critic wrote of a production staged in May 1988, nearly one hundred years after its première, or to shake our heads at an exhibition of maudlin, defeatist, self-pitying sentimentality?

When it comes to a consideration of Yelena it is, once again, the fear of life which seems to characterise her behaviour and, especially, a fear of her own sexual nature. This goes some way towards explaining her decision to marry, at however tender an age, a person one imagines to be some forty years her senior. On the other hand, there seems no need to doubt that the reasons she gives to Sonya for marrying the professor are those she genuinely believes to be true, although she now claims to recognise that the 'real love' has turned out to be 'artificial' (p.28). In fact, her marriage to the professor could be interpreted as a form of spiritual martyrdom designed to protect her from genuine emotional involvement and act as security against sexual feeling. One may even suspect that the marriage remains unconsummated, not only because of the absence of children, but because the relationship between husband and wife is more reminiscent of one between father and daughter.

This is not to say that Yelena is immune to sexual attraction or is unaware of her own attractiveness. At one point she even decides to 'let herself go' (p.54), but her glance into the well of sensuality at this juncture is not followed by a plunge into its depths, as both she and Astrov recoil simultaneously from the shock of emotional connection. However, it would seem to be a mistake to describe her as actively exploiting her allure in the manner of a 'mermaid' (*rusalka*), or the predatory creatures with which she is compared (p.38). She *suffers* things like marriage or attempted seduction to happen. But these actions say as much, if not more, about others as they do about her. The professor's desire to thwart the ageing process by marrying youth, as well as Astrov's desire to prove that he is a virile seducer and not a sad, Vanya-like bachelor, might be said to reveal more about the elderly professor and ageing doctor than they do about the youthful, catalytic figure of Yelena.

The image of Yelena near the beginning of Act One – the adult on a children's swing – is suggestive of a nature which cannot be pinned down with confidence as it veers between opposites – childhood and adulthood, innocence and experience, freedom and security, coming and going. In this last sense, Yelena on the swing might be said to mirror the action of the play itself, based on her arrival at the outset and her departure at the end. Below the advancing and retreating movements of the swing, the embers of suppressed and frustrated feeling are being fanned into life (a Freudian 'return of the repressed') – the literal and emotional tempests of Acts Two and Three seemingly heralded by that sultry, storm-laden afternoon of the play's opening.

Critical views of *Uncle Vanya*

The first important literary critical consideration of *Uncle Vanya* was contained in David Magarshack's study *Chekhov the Dramatist* (1952). He also devoted a good deal of space to the play's forerunner, *The Wood Demon*, which is described as 'essentially a morality play on Tolstoyan lines [. . .] in which vice is converted to virtue' (p.121), and *Uncle Vanya* is also regarded as a play concerned with absolute moral issues of good and evil. Magarshack detects important links between Telegin and Serebryakov, the former acting as a choric figure, 'whose comments on the action heighten the dramatic tension' and who serves as a mirror image of the parasitic professor: 'both of them are spongers [. . .] But intrinsically they are poles apart: the gulf that separates them is that between good and evil' (p.208). He goes on to suggest that a similar contrast between vice and virtue characterises the portrayal of Yelena and Sonya, to the detriment of the former: 'Helen [i.e. Yelena], like her husband, is evil because she is always thinking of herself' (p.220). The contrast is between destructiveness and creativity: 'the incursion of Helen has changed everything [. . .] It is as if a hurricane had swept through their lives and uprooted everything. And it is the young girl's [Sonya's] faith and courage alone that will rebuild the ruins' (p.225).

Magarshack then makes a distinction between absolute moral categories and a specifically social morality when he points to what he describes as 'the idleness, uselessness, and, above all, lack of courage', which characterise the professor and his wife, as opposed to the 'useful work performed by Uncle Vanya, Sonia and Astrov, and, [. . .] their tremendous courage' (p.223). Magarshack sees courage as 'one of the principal themes of the play', exemplified in particular by 'Sonia's deeply moving speech with which the play ends' (ibid.), which contains the suggestion of 'a serene and happy rest after a task well and truly done' (p.224). As proof of its religious seriousness, Magarshack cites the fact that Rakhmaninov felt compelled to set it to music (p.223).

A year later, in 1953, the distinguished American critic, Eric Bentley, described the play as a battleground between creative and destructive impulses, but where the 'destructive passions do not destroy [and] the creative passions do not create'. Both are crushed by 'daily routine [. . .] by boredom and triviality' (p.331). He also sees the play as one in which 'Farce and drama are not eliminated, but subordinated to a higher art', both playing their part 'in the dialectic of the whole' (p.342). He was among the first to note the pattern of arrival and departure which constitutes the action (as, of course, it does in *The Seagull*, *Three Sisters* and *The Cherry Orchard*), and which focuses attention on what happens 'in the short space of time between', and the effect of 'the visit upon the visited' (p.326). He describes the differences between *The Wood Demon* and *Uncle Vanya* as between 'settled' and 'unsettled' fates (which might also be described as 'closed' or 'open' structures). In the earlier play characters die, are paired off, and the play ends happily. In the later play, Chekhov's 'view of the truth' has matured: 'Nobody dies. Nobody is paired off. And the general point is clear: life knows no endings, happy or tragic' (p.325).

Bentley also relates Chekhovian drama to Aristotelian theory and especially the latter's notion of 'anagnorisis' (the moment of tragic perception which is slowly arrived at over the course of the action by the play's protagonist, e.g., Oedipus' eventual discovery of his true identity in *Oedipus Rex*). This produces the realisation that things are not what they have hitherto seemed to be. In Chekhov, by contrast, 'recognition means that what all these years seemed to be so, [. . .] really is so and will remain so', which constitutes a specific kind of Chekhovian recognition. Bentley then compares Chekhov with Ibsen, but where in the work of the latter dramatist, 'the surface of everyday life is a smooth deception [which is] suddenly burst by volcanic eruption', in Chekhov, 'the crust is all too firm; the volcanic energies of men have no chance of emerging' (pp.326–7).

According to Bentley, the 'Might-Have-Been is Chekhov's *idée fixe*' (p.329). 'Astrov's yearnings are not a radical's vision of the future any more than the Professor's doctrine of work is a demand for a worker's state. They are both the daydreams of men who Might Have Been' (pp.340–1). Thus, Astrov is 'to be pitied', while his hope 'that mankind will some day do something good operates as an excuse for doing nothing now' (pp.328–9). His ecological enthusiasms, swiftly abandoned once Yelena arrives on the scene, are nothing 'but an old-maidish hobby, like Persian cats' (p.329), in a play where, 'the surface of everyday life is itself a kind of tragedy' (pp.326–7).

One of the best of the earlier treatments of the play can be found in Maurice Valency's 1966 study, *The Breaking String: The Plays of Anton Chekhov*. Like his discussion of *The Wood Demon*, the critic's view of *Uncle Vanya* focuses on the theme of 'waste' and 'lack of meaning' which, paradoxically, contains 'the deepest meaning of the play' (Valency, 1966, p.185). It is a play in which the action is 'trivial' – a fact highlighted by a simple detail such as the map of Africa in Act Four, which 'throws the whole thing into scale' (p.189). Valency also stresses the link between suffering and living and the fear of life itself. Characters suffer from a disease of the soul characteristic 'of those who do not dare to live' (p.188). There is an inherent conflict between 'desire', which surges periodically to the surface and, 'a tragic lack of energy' to fulfil those desires. It is as if the characters are suffering from a form of 'psychic impotence', where the 'possibility of a more intense experience is apparently more frightening [. . .] than the continuation of the humdrum existence to which they are comfortably committed' (p.187). Each nurses his own characteristic form of the illness and seeks to wrap him- or herself in a protective cover, 'against the elemental blasts of life'.

Valency argues persuasively that Chekhov considered it 'immoral' to thwart nature, 'and worse than immoral to do so under the guise of human obligation'. At the same time, the characters 'are painfully aware of the existence of the outer world', and he identifies the sound of the watchman's rattle as speaking 'eloquently of the security which surrounds them', but also of 'the soul's prison, and the dangers beyond its wall' (p.188). The characters embody contradictory states and impulses. Thus, Yelena, who identifies Astrov as a possible means of escaping a loveless marriage, both desires and rejects this possibility, and 'flies away from him as fast as she can lest something deep and vivid should trouble the calm surface of her boredom' (p.187). The 'external' Vanya, 'is comically inept' in his 'adolescent' pursuit of Yelena, and in his botched attempt to shoot the professor, but 'his ineptitude reveals the depth of his [internal] pain' (p.190). As for Astrov, despite his grandiloquent plans for reforestation and soil-conservation, he 'has no idea what is to be done about the soul-sickness which infects his world' (p.197) from which he also suffers, while Sonya's invocation of a beautiful afterlife is redolent of heartbreak but is, at the same time, a 'child's dream' or a fairy tale (p.203).

Valency also makes the pertinent comparison between this play and Turgenev's *A Month in the Country* and describes the similarities in the forensic terms of a scientific treatise:

> *Uncle Vanya* makes the impression of a vigorous chemical reaction. Into the seemingly stable lives of these country people, there is suddenly introduced a disturbing element, in the nature of a catalyst, and almost at once the whole little world begins to seethe and fume. Ultimately there is something like an explosion. With this display of energy, the disturbing elements are precipitated, the situation regains its equilibrium, and life once again presents its calm and limpid appearance, as if all its tension were dissipated. (p.182)

In an image which suggests a ship that passes in the night of a summer storm, at the final curtain the 'scene recomposes itself as quickly as the sea in the wake of a passing ship' (p.202), following a 'flash of summer lightning [which] has suddenly revealed these lives in all their nakedness' (p.182).

Harvey Pitcher's 1973 study *The Chekhov Play* describes the central theme of the play as 'frustration', brought on by a new scenic character which is 'provincial Russian life itself' (p.75). In fact, if asked to choose one line from the play which exemplified

its spirit, he would cite Astrov's remark to Sonya in Act Two: 'I'm
fond of life as a whole, but this petty, provincial life of ours in
Russia – that I can't stand, I despise it utterly' (p.112). Describing
the difference between *The Wood Demon* and *Uncle Vanya*,
Pitcher notes that 'a play of action' has been replaced by 'a play
of emotional content', especially 'the emotion of frustration', and
attributes this, interestingly, to an evolutionary process which
belongs to both the characters and the distinctive nature of the
play itself:

> One is reminded here of that curious feature of natural evolution,
> whereby it may sometimes be advantageous for a species not to
> proceed to its adult stage of development, but to remain
> permanently in the pre-adult stage, thereby giving rise to an entirely
> new species. A similar process seems to have occurred in the
> evolution of the Chekhov play. *Uncle Vanya* never reaches the
> 'adult' phase of dramatic action and intrigue, but remains
> permanently in the 'pre-adult' phase of emotional processes; and in
> this way a new species of drama came into being. (p.78)

Pitcher also has interesting observations to make about the
significance of 'work' within the scheme of *Uncle Vanya* and the
distinctions between those he describes as 'Givers' and 'Takers'.
Work is described as something Chekhov believed 'should occupy
the central position' in life (p.109), but which in the play is
'something for the characters to fall back on emotionally' out of a
sense of life's frustration (p.86). Characters in the play who are
'Givers' attempt to alleviate human suffering in the process of
working to keep body and soul together, while 'Takers' need to
'satisfy a thirst for glory and self-advertisement' (p.90). The
implication would seem to be that Astrov, Vanya and Sonya
belong to the first category and Serebryakov to the second.
However, in attempting to correct the moralistic over-
simplifications which he believes have characterised some studies of
the play, Pitcher sees Serebryakov as 'not a complete ogre [but] a
genuinely frustrated human being' (p.85), while Astrov pursues
Yelena with 'grim acquiescence rather than romantic yearning
[...] on a level with his vodka-drinking' (p.101). The drinking
has its own equivalence, 'on the mental level', with his faith in a
better future, which is an 'emotional emergency measure adopted
in response to the apparent hopelessness of the present'. Sonya's
recourse, at the end of the play, to 'a poetic and child-like vision

of life after death [. . .] with which to combat present misery'
(p.110), constitutes a similarly evasive strategy.

The theme of work in *Uncle Vanya* is commented on ironically
by Bert O. States, who notes that

> those who preach the philosophy of work in his plays are usually
> sitting down when they do so. [. . .] 'We must work!' usually has
> the character either of a self-admonition or a *plan* for distant
> action, something we needn't do today. [. . .] Thus work, as a
> possible solution to life's ills, is given the character of a chore, as
> opposed to a pride of achievement or what people unavoidably, if
> not cheerfully, do in order to fill their days. (Bert O. States, *The
> Pleasure of the Play*, Ithaca and London, Cornell University Press,
> 1994, pp.171-2)

Laurence Senelick's 1985 study contains a chapter on *Uncle Vanya*
headed by an epigraph from the German philosopher Nietzsche's
work of 1882, *Die Fröhliche Wissenschaft* (*The Gay Science*): 'The
most unendurable thing, to be sure, the really terrible thing, would
be a life without habits, a life which continually required
improvisation' (Senelick, 1985, p.88). Senelick enlarges on this by
citing a quotation from Samuel Beckett's essay on Proust, which
might also serve to characterise *Uncle Vanya*, where 'habit' is
described as a pain-killer designed to anaesthetise 'the perilous
zones in the life of an individual, dangerous, precarious, painful,
mysterious and fertile, when for a moment the boredom of living
is replaced by the suffering of being' (p.97).

Equally valuable are his observations on the language of
oppressiveness in the play, which unites the weather with a human
sense of being choked, or stifled, unable to breathe:

> The more deeply inward the play moves physically, the more the
> sense of oppression mounts. Chekhov uses weather and seasons
> along with certain verbal echoes to produce this feeling. In the first
> few lines of the dialogue, Astrov declares, 'It's stifling' (*dushno*),
> and variations on that sentiment occur with regularity. Vanya
> repeats it and speaks of Yelena's attempt to muffle her youth; the
> Professor begins Act Two by announcing that he cannot breathe,
> and Vanya speaks of being choked by the idea that his life is
> wasted. Astrov admits he would be suffocated if he had to live in
> the house for a month. The two young women fling open windows
> to be able to breathe freely. During the first two acts, a storm is
> brewing and then rages; and Vanya spends the last act moaning,

Tyazhelo menya, [sic] literally, 'It is heavy to me,' or 'I feel weighed down'. At the very end, Sonya's 'We shall rest' (*My otdokhhnyom*) is etymologically related to *dushno* and connotes 'breathing easily' [see note to present edition p. 82]. [. . .] The cumulative effect is one of immobility and stagnation, oppression and frustration. (p.95)

He also notes the significance of time as 'duration' in *Uncle Vanya* where, the 'sense of moments ticking away inexorably is much stronger [. . .] than in Chekhov's other plays', and where the play becomes part of 'a temporal sequence that is only a segment of the entire conspectus of duration' (p.96).

1995 saw the appearance of two studies, one of which, by Donald Rayfield, was the first to be entirely devoted to this play; the other was an extended study of *Uncle Vanya* in the context of Chekhov's other major plays by Richard Gilman, an American critic who had previously discussed Chekhov's work in his *The Making of Modern Drama* (1974). He is the only critic referred to in this section whose discussion appears to be based on English translations of Chekhov.

Donald Rayfield's study is by one of today's leading Chekhov scholars and, as such, essential reading. The monograph runs to some eighty pages, roughly half of which are devoted to *The Wood Demon*, the other half to a close reading of each act of *Uncle Vanya* which, in itself, makes for interesting comparison with J.L. Styan's methods in his *Chekhov in Performance* (1971). The study also includes sections on staging the play, together with its critical reception, and is especially useful in making reference to the director's score of Stanislavsky's original 1899 production, as well as including reproductions of the ground plans of the settings for each act. In common with more recent critics, he reminds us of Chekhov's connections with the later dramatic world of Samuel Beckett, traceable in the 'superbly banal and morbid interchange' during Act One when, in response to Yelena's 'It's nice weather today', there is a pause before Vanya replies, 'It's good weather for hanging yourself' (p.44).

Rayfield also points to the importance of 'time' in the play (p.53), as well as the significance of the absent sister, commented on by Marina who, in his view, has 'a dark side not always noticed by the critics', and who, 'apparently for no good reason', reminds Serebryakov of his deceased wife and of her 'mental and physical agony'. He concludes that 'Restless corpses dominate mature Chekhovian drama' (p.46), which is all of a piece with his sense that 'Uncle Vanya is a play about bereavement: the central characters are cut off from light by the shadow of their beloved dead; Vera Petrovna [the first Mrs Serebryakov], the real love of her brother Voinitsky, has paralysed everyone by her death [...] The role of the absent and of the silent is perhaps what we have so far least understood in Chekhovian drama' (p.74).

Richard Gilman also pursues what is becoming an almost fashionable connection between the dramatic world of Chekhov and that of Samuel Beckett (who are linked by the notion, popularised by the critic Martin Esslin, of a generic 'Theatre of the Absurd'), although Gilman's discussion is rhetorically highly-coloured at times. It is almost as if Chekhov, too, had lived through both World Wars as well as knowing about the Holocaust, the Gulag, Hiroshima and other twentieth-century horrors. He suggests a poetic equivalence between *Uncle Vanya* and Beckett's *Comment c'est* (*How It Is*, 1964) (in which a central character struggles, gulping for air, through a sea of mud). Gilman also cites the example of Beckett's *L'Innommable* (*The Unnamable*, 1952), during the course of which a voice describes the process of 'inching through the ooze' (Gilman, 1995, p.121), as well as the three characters in *Play* (1964) (heads babbling inanities poking from burial urns). Further comparisons are with Winnie, in *Happy Days* (1961), (trapped in a mound of earth and, similarly, engrossed with trivia), and with Vladimir and Estragon in *En Attendant Godot* (*Waiting for Godot*, 1952), abandoned with little solace, 'on a lonely road at evening', who, like all the others, are 'within time where, because of the secret pact among the tenses, it's always too early or too late [and where] the characters of *Uncle Vanya* will know themselves to be in a drama about *how it is* [emphasis added] now' (ibid.).

On a more recognisable, everyday level, Gilman notes the importance of ordinary objects in the play which, as in the work of 'a painter of the "domestic" such as Vermeer', are made to 'give up their secrets', which are 'the secrets also of larger, stranger things' (p.112). In this connection, he mentions things which function 'beyond the logic of narrative and development: the harness-bells, Astrov's glass of vodka, Telegin tuning up and then softly playing his guitar, Marina knitting, Vanya's mother writing in some margin, the watchman tapping, Vanya's calculations on the abacus, sighs, interjections, the candle burning on the table' (p.138). The overall mood of the play is encapsulated for Gilman in Sonya's final speech, where she becomes 'the agent of aesthetic grace', whose words are 'pitched beyond despair and hope', expressing the ' "burden" and "lyricism" of sorrow' (p.139) – a lyricism which 'doesn't transform or redeem the weight of sorrow [but brings] it into intimacy with the soul which, tested by grief, learns about itself ', a grief which 'makes us human', in recognition of a mortality 'which happiness obscures' (p.140).

Production history

Russia and the Soviet Union

Following its first publication in 1897, *Uncle Vanya* was given several performances in the Russian provinces in, among other places, Saratov, Kazan', and in Maxim Gorky's home town, Nizhni-Novgorod. Gorky saw a production there in November, 1898, about which he wrote to Chekhov:

> A few days ago I saw *Uncle Vanya* [. . .] and I wept like an old woman. [. . .] as I watched the actors I felt I was being sawn through with a blunt saw. Its teeth penetrate straight to the heart. [. . .] Your *Uncle Vanya* is a completely new type of dramatic art, a hammer with which you strike the empty pates of the public. [. . .] Only what do you mean to achieve by such blows? Will they bring man back to life? True, we are wretched people, 'tedious' people, gloomy, repulsive people, and one has to be a monster of virtue to love and pity the bags of guts we are and to try and help us to live. Yet, all the same, people are to be pitied. [. . .] You know, it seems to me that in this play you are colder to people than the devil himself. You are as indifferent to them as the snow, as a blizzard. (Maxim Gorky, *Letters*, ed. P. Cockerell, Moscow, Progress Publishers, 1966, pp.15–16)

In the wake of the Moscow Art Theatre's successful production of *The Seagull,* in December 1898, Nemirovich-Danchenko approached Chekhov with a request to be allowed to follow this up with a production of *Uncle Vanya.* However, Chekhov had already been asked by A.M. Kondrat'ev, artistic director of the Moscow Maly Theatre, for permission to stage the play and so Chekhov felt obliged to let him have first refusal. The Maly's literary-theatrical committee met on 8 April 1899, when the play was subjected to criticism and demands that changes be made.

Chekhov was offended and, without more ado, he handed the play
to the Art Theatre where it opened on 26 October that same year.
Chekhov attended a few rehearsals during the summer and replied
to letters from Knipper and others about points of interpretation
(see Worrall, 1986, pp.46–8). He saw the eventual production
when it toured Sebastopol in the spring of 1900 and liked it better
than he had *The Seagull*.

Stanislavsky prepared a detailed production score, as he had for
The Seagull. All in all, there are 800 numbered notes over the
four acts in a proportion of 164:219:244:172. His approach is
extremely naturalistic, pedantically so at times, even specifying the
precise number of knives and forks on the table in Act Two;
requesting a live chicken in Act One and asking for wire netting to
be placed along the front of the stage to prevent it escaping into
the auditorium. Vanya's mother is even given a lapdog, from
which she is never parted.

The first act is dominated by mosquitoes, which the characters
are to imagine arriving in swarms from the 'pine forest' in which
Stanislavsky imagines the action taking place, and which they swat
continually. Astrov is given a long cigarette holder as a permanent
prop, rolls his own cigarettes, and is discovered sitting on a
squeaky swing reading a book. Marina is given a hearing problem.
The score is full of detailed activity. For example, at one point
Astrov gets up from the swing, shakes himself, combs his
moustache and hair and re-ties his tie. During his speech about the
shunter who died on the operating table he is described as
smoking thoughtfully and flicking the ash off his cigarette so as to
hit the ground at one and the same spot, or, possibly 'if it doesn't
seem too crude' spitting at the same spot with equal accuracy (K.S.
Stanislavskii, *Rezhisserskie ekzempliary K.S. Stanislavskogo
1898–1930*, '*Diadia Vania*' *A.P. Chekhova 1899g.*, ed. I.N.
Solov'eva, Moscow-St Petersburg, Atheneum-Feniks, 1994,
pp.7–11).

Vanya swats mosquitoes from the moment he enters while
Telegin is required to wipe his forehead, hair and neck, shake his
jacket to get the creases out of the back, take out a watch, listen
to it, take a key out of his purse and wind it '(the watch is a
silver one)', listen to it and replace it carefully in his pocket (p.15).
Vanya places a handkerchief over his head as protection against
mosquitoes (p.17). Astrov jots down the name of the plants in
plant pots in a notebook (p.15) and then serves himself

strawberries and cream with sugar (p.17). Marina chases a chicken
with a wooden switch (p.23). Sonya strokes the dog which her
grandmother is clutching, plays with it, feeds it bits of bread. 'In
the pauses the noise of the stroking needs to be heard and it
would be good if the dog barked,' adds Stanislavsky (p.25). Astrov
and Vanya take it in turns to push Yelena on the swing, the one
standing in front of her, the other behind.

Act Three opens with Yelena and Sonya playing a duet for four
hands on the piano with Vanya conducting (p.67). During Yelena's
soliloquy, prior to her scene over the maps with Astrov, she
accompanies herself at the piano and is described in the score as a
'rusalka' (a water nymph) (p.75). Her flirtation with Astrov is
unambiguously portrayed as she 'coquettishly' leans against the
window frame and permits him to hold her hand, her
'embarrassment' being merely 'a mask' (p.79). During his wooing,
Astrov chases Yelena about the stage. She takes refuge behind the
piano (p.83). During the scene of the family council, there occurs
what Stanislavsky describes as a 'narodnaia stsena' (a public
rumpus):

> All begin to kick up a racket. The dog barks. Sonya hurls herself in
> Yelena's path who collapses onto the divan in a semi-hysterical
> state. Sonya brings her water and fusses over her. Maria Vasilyevna
> stands behind an armchair as a sort of barricade, waves her arms
> at Voinitsky and shrieks at him, 'Listen to Aleksandr!' Marina flaps
> a stocking at them as if at fighting cocks and keeps repeating
> something over and over. Behind the columns, Telegin rushes about
> as if the place was on fire, shouting something. Voinitsky howls,
> slumped against the stove and cradling himself in his arms. Howls,
> cries, screams. Serebryakov sits like a stuffed dummy, gesturing
> nervously. (p.97)

This is followed by a further 'narodnaia stsena' after the first shot
has been fired:

> A general cry. Voinitsky shouts and lunges after Serebryakov.
> Yelena screams, clinging to Voinitsky's arm. Telegin runs backwards
> waving his arms and moaning. Serebryakov runs in and backs
> against the wall. Sonya tries to stop Serebryakov [presumably
> Stanislavsky means Voinitsky] and screams. Marina huddles in a
> corner afraid of the pistol shots; Maria Vasilyevna is on the divan,
> the dog has leapt from her arms and runs about the stage. (p.101)

For the Act Four setting the number of bird cages is increased to three, one in each of three windows (p.105). The scene of farewell between Yelena and Astrov is elaborately choreographed. Astrov

> takes her by the right hand and, with his left, turns her to face him and, bending his head forward, gives her a prolonged kiss, and, at the end of the kiss, grabs her passionately around the waist without releasing her right hand. Yelena tries to break away from him while he continues to embrace her. [...] Passionately (only once before during her lifetime had Yelena experienced such a kiss) she embraces Astrov, presses herself against him, like a water nymph. Astrov, in danger of losing his head and fearing loss of self-control tears himself free of her embrace. (p.119)

When Knipper described this interpretation to Chekhov, he felt obliged to offer his own thoughts on the matter by way of a corrective: Astrov 'talks to her in this scene in the same tone as he speaks of the heat in Africa, and kisses her quite simply for want of anything better to do. If Astrov conducts this scene in a violent fashion then the whole quiet and listless mood of Act Four will be lost' (letter to Olga Knipper, 30 September 1899).

Just before the curtain closed 'slowly and quietly' at the end, the audience were treated to a mixture of atmospheric sounds – Sonya's barely audible murmuring of a prayer; Vanya's weeping; the beating of rain on the window pane; a 'ceremoniously-mournful' tune from Telegin's guitar (as opposed to the 'strumming' which Chekhov asks for); Marina's snoring (not the sounds of her knitting); the sound of Maria Vasilyevna reading in a monotone and the noise of pages being turned; the chirring of a cricket (p.133).

It took time for the production to find favour with audiences but, in an attempt to reassure Chekhov, his boyhood friend Aleksandr Vishnevsky, who played Vanya, described the second night's performance as 'a thousand times better than *The Seagull*' (A.P. Kuzicheva, *A.P. Chekhov v russkoi teatral'noi kritike – Kommentirovannaia antologia 1887–1917*, Moscow, Chekhovskii poligraficheskii kombinat, 1999, p.181). A critic writing in the *Stock Exchange Gazette & News*, on 6 November, was perplexed by the insignificance of the central character but thought that Chekhov had hit on something altogether new as both a symbolist and impressionist. The play was 'a mood in four acts' (p.178); the roles had been brilliantly allocated and the production itself expressed a feeling of 'brotherly love' for Chekhov. It also showed evidence of an immense amount of work, resulting in a production entirely in keeping with the mood of the work and 'deserving of the highest, most enthusiastic praise' (p.180).

A Petersburg critic, Yuri Beliaev, saw the production twice in Moscow but waited until it toured before reviewing it. In his snobbish opinion:

> The troupe possesses no single actor of talent, apart from Mr Stanislavsky [...] The task of the production goes no further than the subjugation of the actor's personality to the ensemble. The actors, in the absence of talent and personal initiative are forced simply to gaze into the director's eyes, obey his instructions, keep time and hold the pauses. Thus, for the sake of lifelikeness, they are required to catch mosquitoes, yawn as realistically as possible, cough when others are talking and blow their noses as need be. [...] The only authentic person on the stage in my view was Mr Stanislavsky because he has talent, because he doesn't listen to anybody apart from himself and because he actually lives on stage. I observed him yesterday as he played Dr Astrov. An absolutely living person, when others are only copies. [...] Uncle Vanya is emphasised by lack of restraint and clamour [...] Dr Astrov is a similarly expiring member of the intelligentsia [...] but with an inescapable spiritual anguish which forces him to tipple. The professor is given all the outlines of a talentless Faust [...] having found his Margarita in the person of Yelena [...] Miss Knipper is insignificant as Yelena Andreevna although from an external point of view it would be difficult to find a more suitable artist. Miss Lilina depicts Sonya touchingly, as does Mr Artem Telegin. [...] A small observation on the part of directorial niceties. There are plenty in the production, but one in particular sticks out. This has to do with the curtains shaken by the wind, only one of which does so while the other one hangs as if nothing is happening. Moreover the curtain billows outwards from the room as if the dining room was windy and the yard outside as quiet as anything. This is, of course, a minor matter. But Mr Stanislavsky ought to know, all the same, which way the wind blows. (pp.214–15)

The production proved popular during the Theatre's first three seasons but, by 1923, had only been given a total of 192 performances. There were no further productions of the play at the Moscow Art Theatre until 1947.

Meyerhold staged *Uncle Vanya* in Kherson in 1902 – a production characterised by the excessive naturalism which he had absorbed at the Art Theatre – and again in Poltava, in 1906, when a critic drew important distinctions between Meyerhold's developing methods and those of the company he had abandoned four years earlier:

> At the Art Theatre they strive towards an extraordinary photographic transmission of all the details, seek to embody the truth of reality on stage. V.E. Meyerhold strives to attain artistic truth. This artistic truth is not reached through the painstaking reproduction of each detail but with several bold brushstrokes, which underline and strengthen the impression which, in the artist's view, should completely captivate the spectator. Meyerhold embodies the principles of impressionism on stage. (p.412)

According to the Art Theatre's most recent literary manager, Mikhail Kedrov's 1947 production 'was an attempt to interpret the play in the optimistic spirit of Socialist Realism [...] that threw the theatre back to pre-Chekhovian times', devoid of ensemble but with a splendid central performance by Boris Dobronravov as Vanya (Anatoly Smeliansky, 'Chekhov at the Moscow Art Theatre', in Gottlieb and Allain, 2000, p.32). The production was included in the company's visit to London, in 1958, when Dmitri Orlov replaced Dobronravov in the role of Vanya. It was seen at the Sadler's Wells Theatre by the influential critic of the *Observer*, Kenneth Tynan, who described it as follows:

> On the surface this Vanya is a man of weight and substance. [...] Only in flashes do we glimpse the man within, an adolescent who can neither be his age nor live up to his looks. It is a lightweight who peers out through the pale eyes of the heavyweight face. [...] Dignity never deserts him. He clings to it even in the shooting spree, which becomes in its mad way a matter of honour, an assertion of principle rather than a display of temperament; and in tenacity like this there is a kind of heroism. Mr Orlov's clumsy nobility puts us in mind [...] of Don Quixote. This Vanya always looks capable of tragedy: his tragedy is that he is capable only of comedy. [...] But the true stars of the show [...] are the second-act storm and the dawn that succeeds it. [...] It begins far off, with a premonitory rumble and a hiss of light rain. The curtains faintly billow. Then with a catarrhal explosion that makes the theatre throb, it is upon us: the curtains flare like flags,

and the rain pelts down, so savagely that we can hear it splashing off the porch into its own puddles. (Kenneth Tynan, *Curtains*, Longmans, Green & Co., 1961, pp.437–8)

Georgi Tovstonogov's 1982 production, staged at the Leningrad Bolshoi Drama Theatre, travelled to Edinburgh in August 1987, for the Festival. It was a 'gloriously funny production', that found 'humour in every angst-ridden line [...] a delightful picture of the silliness and petulance of grown men' (Sarah Hemmings, *Independent* 14 August 1987). Oleg Basilashvili, as Vanya, had a 'dandified habit of tugging at his absurdly large cravat', and dragged 'his large body across the stage like a somnambulistic bear' (Michael Billington, *Guardian*, 14 August 1987), while at times looking 'like a crazed Spike Milligan' (Peter France, *TLS*, 28 August 1987). Kirill Lavrov, as Astrov, emphasised his indifference to Sonya by putting his arm round her in a 'playfully jocular way', and squashing a hat on her head during their night-time scene together in Act Two. The scene between Astrov and Yelena over the maps in Act Three was played as comedy 'with Astrov almost enveloping Elena, gazing brazenly at her hair and face, and incongruously proffering her a magnifying glass to peruse his sketches' (Gordon McVay, *THES*, 28 August 1987). Evgeni Lebedev's Serebryakov was 'a spruce little peacock who treats the universe as if it were created for his convenience' (Billington, op. cit.). Before the scene of the family council, Vanya entered with his bunch of autumn roses to find Yelena in the arms of Astrov. Searching in desperate embarrassment for somewhere to get rid of the bouquet, he abandoned it on a table only for Serebryakov to enter, pick it up and give it the approving sniff of one convinced the bouquet was meant for himself. He then continued to hold on to it, even when being pursued by Vanya, comically shielding his head from the bullet with the bunch of roses, and keeping a wary eye on his assailant by squinting through the stems. The pistol shot itself had been preceded by a piece of comic business with 'Vanya pausing to check that his pistol is loaded, turning his head away from his target before firing, and preening himself on his successful marksmanship before realizing that he has managed to miss yet again' (McVay, op.cit.).

Oleg Yefremov's 1985 Moscow Art Theatre production was chiefly remarkable for the sets by V.Ya. Levental and Innokenti Smoktunovski's performance as Vanya. According to Smeliansky:

Levental had placed the house upstage against the background of an autumnal landscape in the style of Levitan [a nineteenth-century Russian landscape painter]. When the stage was plunged into darkness, we suddenly noticed through the mist a faint light suspended above the dewy ground. It was a small window in a house on a distant hill. The light shone dimly in the darkness, but it shone invitingly, showing the way. Such was the end of the performance, premièred on the very eve of changes that were to transform not only Russia but the entire world. (Gottlieb and Allain, 2000, p.37)

When the production was seen at the National Theatre, London, in 1989, critics were more or less unanimously approving, apart from the occasional dissenting voice which saw 'the actors carrying their burdens of despair like heavy knapsacks [in] a mood almost as glum as a light comedy conceived by Samuel Beckett' (Milton Shulman, *Evening Standard*, 15 September 1989). For Michael Ratcliffe, writing in the *Observer*, Smoktunovski's was a 'magnificent performance' pitched 'halfway between senility and childhood, distracted by the pointlessness of his existence [and covering] his head with his hands to fend off blows to come like a man who cannot wait for eternity and wished he had never been born' (17 September 1989). For Paul Taylor, the *Independent on Sunday* theatre critic, the production took its cue from Levental's 'superb set', which kept 'opening up, sliding round, and moving into new alignments. [. . .] Elegiac and entertaining, forlorn and mellow, Chekhov's great tragic-comedy of torpor is, in this production, wonderfully vivified' (16 September 1989). For the *Guardian* critic, Michael Billington, there were two memorable moments in particular: 'One was the precision of the sound-effects so that even the rainstorm alternates between melancholy gusts and a harsh, hail-like patter. The other is the sight of the great Smoktunovski stirring from a life of illusions to confront reality so that even the tub of exquisite, autumn roses he once proffered Yelena is finally given a violently emphatic boot' (18 September 1989).

British productions

The first production of *Uncle Vanya* in Britain was given by the Stage Society at the Aldwych Theatre, London, on 11 May 1914. It was described by Desmond MacCarthy as a 'real tragedy', with the 'flatness and poignancy of life itself' (Desmond MacCarthy, *Drama*, London and New York, Putnam, 1940, p.123), with characters 'like those loosely agglutinated sticks and straws which revolve together slowly in some sluggish eddy' (p.125). While Chekhov's intellectuals appear 'half dead', the other half of them 'is very much, painfully much, alive', suffering as they do 'from an unduly protracted youth' (pp.125–6). This was followed, in November 1921, by a production staged by the Russian émigré director, Fyodor (Theodore) Komisarjevsky, at the Royal Court Theatre, London, which he revived at the Barnes Theatre, Surrey, in January 1926. An unsigned notice in the *Morning Post* described the characters as having 'the simplicity and directness of children', who are, 'not in an abusive sense . . . infantile' (Emeljanow, 1981, p.295). It was a 'wonderful play' wonderfully acted, for which the producer could take all the credit (*Daily Herald*, cited in Emeljanow, p.298). There followed productions at the Birmingham Repertory Theatre, in April 1927, directed by W.G. Fay who had been associated with Yeats and the Abbey Theatre, Dublin; by the touring Prague Group, performed in Russian and directed by Maria Germanova at the Garrick Theatre, London, in April 1928; at the Westminster Theatre, London, in February 1937, directed by Michael Maccowan; and at the New Theatre, London, in January 1945, directed by John Burrell and with Sybil Thorndike, Laurence Olivier and Ralph Richardson. Describing this last, the critic Alan Dent wrote:

> The play is a picture of pre-Revolutionary provincial Russia – full of dankness, gloom, frustration, tedium, thwarted ambitions run to seed, and young love most bitterly unrequited. Everybody at the end is drooping, disheartened; and you come away from it – such is the paradox of these masterpieces when beautifully interpreted as here – heartened, radiant, exhilarated. (Alan Dent, *Nocturnes and Rhapsodies*, London, Hamish Hamilton, 1951, p.54)

Olivier himself revived *Uncle Vanya* at the Chichester Festival Theatre, in 1962, which then transferred to the National Theatre at the Old Vic, in November 1963. For Kenneth Tynan, the play illustrated the fact that 'There is a tide in the affairs of men; and Chekhov's people have all missed it'. The production contained two 'superlative performances' – by Olivier (who also directed) as Astrov, and by Michael Redgrave as Vanya (Kenneth Tynan, *Tynan Right and Left*, London, Longmans, 1967, p.110). Harold

Clurman saw it on tour in New York when he found the play had been 'given a thoroughly understanding production' in which the last two acts were 'especially moving. Redgrave is brilliant in the scene where he bursts out against his selfish pedant of a brother-in-law, and in his final grief, inconsolable'. However the production itself he felt was rather mannered.

> In this production one recognizes a company of meticulous actors who have gone reverently to work. But for Chekhov, sound craftsmanship, even dramatic intelligence, are not enough. This *Uncle Vanya* lacks, not entirely, but enough to leave me a little dissatisfied, the true core of the play – that palpable *idealism* which is at the heart of Chekhov's writing [...] Thus Rosemary Harris, exquisite as the beauty gone to waste, seems more like an affected bluestocking than a richly endowed woman in whom the sap of life is slowly evaporating. The effect is unintentionally comic, but not comic in Chekhov's way, which is never the least brittle or even faintly depreciatory. Redgrave's Vanya, on the other hand, might assume more comic meaning in the correct sense if he were less the stifled intellectual at the outset [...] and more the flustered, slightly dishevelled, self-neglecting dreamer going to seed. The visual sign of what I have indicated is the stylized plain wood setting [by Sean Kenny], which is an abstraction of nothing. It suggests hardly any place either actual or symbolic – only a kind of literal dead end, wholly juiceless. The loneliness and ennui of Chekhov's world may be stultifying, but they are never dry. (Harold Clurman, *The Naked Image: Observations on the Modern Theatre*, London and New York, Collier Macmillan, 1966, pp.190–1)

A production was staged at the Oxford Playhouse, directed by Frank Hauser, in April 1969, followed by another at London's Royal Court Theatre, in 1970, with Paul Scofield, especially memorable, according to J.C. Trewin, for the quality of his vocal delivery with 'its dragging emphasis [and] atypical downbeat throb on the last syllable'. The moment in Act Three, when 'he stood holding his useless bouquet of autumn roses [...] murmuring "Not to worry ... !" ', was delivered entirely in character and seemed like a hopeless understated 'description of a wrecked liner as a "boating accident" (cited in Garry O'Connor, *Paul Scofield: The Biography*, London, Sidgwick & Jackson, 2002, p.238). October 1973 saw a revival at the Bristol Old Vic, with Peter O'Toole as Vanya, but it was Nicol Williamson's performance of

the same role which claimed greater critical attention, in
December 1974, at the Royal Shakespeare Company's 'fringe'
venue, The Other Place, in Stratford-upon-Avon. According to
Michael Billington, Williamson presented 'an extraordinary
spectacle of the spirit of a child inhabiting the body of a grown
man'. During the family council scene, he directed 'short, nervous,
stabbing gestures at the Professor' and 'aimless kicks like a
thwarted infant'. When contemplating himself as a frustrated
Dostoevsky, or a Schopenhauer, his body language and bulging
eyes conveyed a feeling of 'temporary insanity'. This was 'superb
acting; and, as in all good Chekhov, the audience is caught
between laughter and tears' (Michael Billington, *One Night Stands*,
London, Nick Hern Books, p.59).

In a 1977 production at the Royal Exchange Theatre,
Manchester, Leo McKern played Vanya as a 'great Russian bear of
a man lolloping around the stage propelled by an uncertain
mixture of hope and despair and forever bouncing off the sharper
corners of the other characters until they finally pierce his skin and
he is deflated' (Sheridan Morley, *Shooting Stars – Plays and
Players 1975–1983*, London, Quartet Books, 1983, pp.79–80). In
the same production, Albert Finney's Astrov was described as
resembling 'a great bull who was finding the social code of the
china shop hard to observe' (Benedict Nightingale, *The Times*, 22
February 1992). This production was slightly more successful than
one given in November 1979, at London's Hampstead Theatre, in
a version by Pam Gems, directed by Nancy Meckler, with Nigel
Hawthorne as Vanya and Ian Holm as Astrov. It was a production
which Arthur Schmidt thought had not been directed so much as
'sedated'. This *Uncle Vanya* was 'quite literally overcast, its
performance not so much paced as spaced out', and for which
Alison Steadman's Sonya had 'disinterred' Joan Crawford's
shoulders in an overwrought interpretation of the role. Nigel
Hawthorne did 'most with least' in managing to make 'yearning as
physical an act as walking'. Altogether, the production was 'a
diffuse effort, splayed under the weight of badly used talent' (*Plays
and Players*, February 1980, p.29).

1982 saw two revivals – the first in May on the National
Theatre's Lyttelton proscenium stage, directed by Michael
Bogdanov; the second, in August, at the London Haymarket
Theatre, directed by Christopher Fettes. Michael Bryant seemed too
old for Vanya in Bogdanov's production, while Patti Love's Sonya

appeared 'clownish [...] simple, peasant-like [...] with a touch
of the holy fool', an unlikely daughter for Serebryakov and no
possible wife for Astrov. Dinsdale Landen gave 'a powerful,
magnetic performance' as Astrov, and conveyed 'his growing
coarseness, booziness and desperation' (Richard Findlater, *Plays
and Players*, July 1982, pp.24–5). Fettes, according to Frank
Marcus, treated the play 'operatically', in a banal production
which 'seemed to have as its sole purpose the display of virtuosity
as a character actor of the protean Donald Sinden [who gave] the
impression of a clever and skilful actor searching frantically for
clues and clutching desperately at comic and pathetic straws'. The
production was 'disastrously miscast', apart from Harry Andrews's
Serebryakov, which was 'the one unqualified success [...] His
couple of seconds' hesitation before he is convinced that the
second bullet has indeed missed him – very slightly disappointing
the hypochondriac in him – is an example of comic bravura of a
high order in an otherwise dull and dispiriting evening' (*Plays and
Players*, October 1982, pp.26–7).

Critics were happier with Michael Blakemore's revival at the
Vaudeville Theatre, London, in 1988, with Michael Gambon as a
bulky, crumpled Vanya, staggering through the play like a punch-
drunk fighter. Michael Billington admired his 'brilliant monument
to ineffectuality', as well as Jonathan Pryce's Astrov, played as 'the
might-have-been'. At the end, 'with Vanya and Sonya together at
the work-table and with her cradling his great baby's head in her
arms', Billington felt 'the poignancy of starting life again on the
flat', when, as Desmond MacCarthy had described it, 'a few hours
before it has run shrieking up the scale of pain' (*Guardian*, 26
May 1988). T.J. Binyon was more sceptical. Noting that the
production gave a first outing for the present, 'spare, lean and
colloquial translation' by Michael Frayn, it also eliminated 'all the
old elegiac melancholy' in favour of a 'hearty, robust, even
knockabout style'. At the beginning of Act One, Astrov and
Marina 'hurtle[d] out of their starting blocks and into the text
with the obvious intention of taking half an hour or so off the
world record for a performance of the play' and despite 'some
magnificent moments', the 'overall impression [was] that of a
number of people meeting at a bus station', with nothing in
common, 'apart from the fact that they are all travelling in the
same direction' (T.J. Binyon, *TLS*, 10 June 1988).

At the Bristol Old Vic, in 1990, Timothy West played Vanya as 'a peevish, overgrown schoolboy, a lugubrious buffoon burning with short-fused jealous fury', his voice breaking, 'whenever he remembers his beloved dead sister', and caressing and kissing a closed piano when 'imagining marital bliss with Yelena' (Gordon McVay, *Plays and Players*, December 1990, p.36). This was succeeded by a revival, staged by the Renaissance Theatre Company in August 1991, at the Lyric Theatre Hammersmith, directed by Kenneth Branagh and Peter Egan. According to Zinovy Zinik, the production 'translated the play into the language of European culture, with a clear Calvinist stress on the sense of doom and grim predestination that surrounds our sinful, futile existence. Sonya's exhortations to work [...] are here presented with the masochistic tear of joy of one who is glad to be back in the dreary routine of eternal earthly damnation' (*TLS*, 3 August 1991, p.17). In the family council scene, a lighter note was introduced when Richard Briers' Vanya 'almost bursts with indignation and forces a fight [with Serebryakov] in which the two lock chair legs over the dining table like stags in rut' (Graham Hassell, *Plays and Players*, October 1991, p.37).

Among the best productions of the 1990s was that staged by Sean Mathias in the National Theatre's intimate Cottesloe auditorium. As T.J. Binyon noted, it was a rather idiosyncratic interpretation:

> When Doctor Astrov (Anthony Sher) strides on to the stage at the opening of the play in filthy breeches and sweat-stained shirt, takes off his spurs and buries a mud-caked face in the lap of Marina, the old nurse (Antonia Pemberton), it becomes obvious that we are not going to see a conventional production of *Uncle Vanya* [...] People hug one another more often, and with less restraint, than the participants of a riotous group therapy session: this is perhaps not surprising, given Uncle Vanya's (Ian McKellan) obvious need of treatment. Having failed to shoot Serebryakov (Eric Porter), he curls into a foetal ball, and in the next act gets into bed fully dressed and hugs a pillow. Yet none of this obscures the fact that this is a fine and exciting production. (*TLS*, 6 March 1992)

Irving Wardle described a 'drunken Astrov hunting for Yelena [Janet McTeer] under the dining-room table, where his game is stopped short by discovering Serebryakov's hoard of pills', and who, at another moment, 'moans with pleasure as Sonya feeds him cheese', and who agrees to stop drinking 'by taking one last

drink'. Other aspects of character were revealed when, for
example, Yelena's aloofness thawed, 'to reveal a depth of
unhappiness far beyond the standard picture of indolent
melancholy', and Serebryakov was transformed from 'a peevish
pedant into a pugnacious sacred monster, finally bidding Vanya
farewell with a magnanimous handclasp which will silence his
enemy for ever' (*Independent on Sunday*, 1 March 1992).

1996 saw a production by Bill Bryden, at the Minerva Theatre,
Chichester, with Derek Jacobi and an all-star cast, which then
transferred to the Albery Theatre in London. Mike Poulton's
'attention-seeking translation' had Astrov describing Vanya and
himself as 'irascible old farts', and Yelena as having 'a "To Let"
sign hanging on her brain' (Lyn Gardner, *Guardian*, 20 September
1996). Benedict Nightingale enthused over the qualities of the cast:
'If Alec Guinness were to turn up as the chap who brings Dr
Astrov his tipple, or the late Henry Irving was the night
watchman, one would hardly be surprised' (*The Times*, 11 July
1996). Michael Billington praised Trevor Eve's 'lank-haired, vodka-
swilling' Astrov, Imogen Stubbs' manipulative, mesmerising, slightly
neurotic Yelena, and Derek Jacobi's cherubic Vanya. Frances
Barber was a more sensual Sonya than usual, who licked her hand
after it had been kissed by Astrov, while Alec McGowan's 'stick-
wielding tyrant' of a Serebryakov (replaced by Richard Johnson
after the transfer), revealed another side to his nature when being
'coddled and soothed' like a child by Peggy Mount's 'earthy and
sympathetic nurse' (*Guardian*, 10 July 1996).

The first British production of *Uncle Vanya* in this century was
by Greg Hersov at the Manchester Royal Exchange Theatre, in
September 2001, with Tom Courtenay as Vanya. Courtenay based
his interpretation on a child-like frailty he discovered in the role
and which he brought to bear on its physical realisation, walking
with an uncertain stagger 'like some wind-up top on rough
ground, or a child off its balance in a newly big world' while
behaving like 'a boy wanting to join in grown-up games' (Jeremy
Kingston, *The Times*, 12 September 2001). A production directed
by Sam Mendes at the Donmar Warehouse, London, in 2002,
described itself rather immodestly as 'by Brian Friel. A version of
the play by Anton Chekhov'. This 'version' enlarged the role of
Telegin, who was given a running gag in which he expressed his
admiration for Germans and another about perspiration, asking
Yelena at one point whether she tended to sweat a lot (*Plays and*

Players, October/November 2002, p.9). Nobody seemed to madden Simon Russell Beale's Vanya more than his 'smugly intellectual uncaring mother', which made Benedict Nightingale 'feel in him a frustration that began in the pram and only now has reached meltdown' (*The Times*, 18 September 2002).

American and other productions

The first production of *Uncle Vanya* in the United States was that of the Moscow Art Theatre on tour at Jolson's Theatre, New York, on 24 May 1924. A rather unworldly critic in *World* compared the play to 'old time melodrama thrillers of the American stage', whose action 'centers about the emotional torment through which a homely young woman passes in the course of her association with a handsome doctor' who, in his turn, is 'ignorant of the girl's affection, but is in love with a second lady who has determined to plead the unfortunate girl's case for her'. Stanislavsky's performance as Astrov was described as 'one of the most appealing' he had given (Emeljanow, 1981, p.258). The first English-language production was directed by Jed Harris, at New York's Cort Theatre, in April 1930, with Lilian Gish as Yelena. It produced mixed responses, ranging from Robert Liddell's feeling that this was 'the finest of Chekhov's plays' (p.365) to Brooks Atkinson's characterisation of the play as 'the least interesting of Chekhov's major dramas' (p.366). However, Atkinson also considered it a 'finely wrought production [. . .] full of pale, tender beauty – and humor' (p.367). Critics were struck by the fact that Chekhov was not all doom and gloom although the extremely free translation hardly bore this out. Apart from filling in Chekhov's pauses and adding dialogue, it even inserted elaborate stage directions, such as this final one to Act Four: '[Sonya] weeps passionately, agonizedly. This is the suffering about which, in that future, she will speak to God. This, and not the other, is the truth. And so she weeps' (Senelick, 1997, p.181).

David Ross revived the play at New York's Fourth Street Theatre, in 1956, with Franchot Tone as Astrov. Eric Bentley commented: 'Error compounded with error yields results, of course, and one of them is a 'comic' Chekhov with the juice drained away, the juice of urgent emotion and serious significance' (*What is Theatre?*, London, Methuen, 1969, p.288). The next major revival of the play was by Mike Nichols, at the New York

Circle in the Square Theatre, in 1973, with Nicol Williamson,
George C. Scott, and an all-star cast. However, according to
Stanley Kauffmann, Nichols 'proved a poor astronomer' (*Persons
of the Drama*, New York and London, Harper & Row, 1976,
p.148). Julie Christie as Yelena had 'all the impact of a faded
fashion model', while Sonya's final speech, as delivered by
Elizabeth Wilson, was 'a tear bath that would float a cruiser'
(p.147). George C. Scott was 'poor, not even magnificently poor,
as Astrov'. The production's one saving grace was Nicol
Williamson who, as Vanya, gave an 'impressive performance
[. . .] he has a vision of Vanya, as a man with abilities and with
shackles [. . .] a good mind and a poor ability to advance his
ideas' (p.148).

Andrei Serban's 1983 production, staged in New York with the
La MaMa troupe and a cast headed by Joseph Chaikin, was
considered rather eccentric in conception, dominated by an
enormous set by Loquasto, 'a sprawling, multi-level house, a maze
of corridors, rooms, stairways, covering a rectangular playing
space some 50 feet by 20.' A sunken cellar in the centre served as
Vanya's study, in what amounted to a surreal environment where
characters were 'like rats in a trap' [. . .] At one moment, Sonya
suddenly ran two laps around the space, before sinking abjectly to
her knees' (Allen, 2000, p.141). In the family council scene in Act
Three, following Serebryakov's revelation of his plans for the
estate, instead of flying into a rage, Vanya crossed the stage and
clambered on to the professor's knee, 'like a child, cuddling him
and smiling, and speaking to him in a soft sing-song voice', which
bemused most critics but was interpreted by one as expressing
'hatred boiled down to its sarcastic essence' (p.142). In 1991,
André Gregory held a series of open rehearsals of the play, at the
Victory Theatre, New York, in a version by David Mamet, which
gave rise to an interesting film, directed by Louis Malle, *Vanya on
42nd Street*. This revealed a very Stanislavskyan, low-key,
naturalistic approach to the acting but, sustaining the idea of a
rehearsal, was performed without any accompanying theatrical
clutter. Finally, the Irondale Ensemble Project collaborated with the
St Petersburg Salon Theatre, between 1985 and 1990, on a version
of the play which dismantled it 'into a demented collage of
vaudeville bits concerning a Michigan radio host who thinks he is
Chekhov's hero'. This work-in-progress 'was a deliberate grafting of
pop on to what was perceived as high art' (Senelick, 1997, p.183).

One of the most striking productions of *Uncle Vanya* staged during the past twenty years was that of Eimunas Nekrosius, at the Lithuanian State Theatre in 1986, and which was awarded a USSR State Prize. The production, according to Michael Billington, amounted to a condemnation of the characters as 'vain, vulgar, foolish and historically irrelevant'. It began:

> with Astrov warming his medical cupping-glasses over a lambent flame; it ends, symmetrically enough, with Sonya applying these self-same purifying glasses to a distraught Vanya's back. Great play is also made of a pair of leaden weights which the enfeebled, symbolically impotent Professor vainly tries to lift. Yet, for all their debility, these characters have feral, predatory urges. Astrov (the great ecologist) periodically dons an animal-hide and prowls around the stage emitting savage grunts and even Yelena at one stage sports the kind of moth-eaten fur you associate with old ladies in gin-palaces. [Nekrosius] turns it into a bitter farce about a doomed class openly derided by their servants. [He] introduces three menials as both a running-gag and choric commentators skating about the floor in dust-removing shoes, nicking unwanted food and cigarettes and mimicking their employers' undignified misery. [...] Yelena, for instance, is played as a roguish tease [...] While the professor outlines his plan to sell the estate, the family poses for a group photo with the servants while they all join in humming *Va pensiero* from *Nabucco*: haunting but stunningly irrelevant since it is a song sung by captive Hebrews pining for their homeland. And Sonya's great confession to Yelena of her love for the doctor is played with brimming tears to the sound of insistent melancholy organ chords. [In a production full of ostentatious oddities] Astrov's maps of the forest here become minute postage-stamps viewed through a huge, magnifying lens. (Michael Billington, *Guardian*, 3 October 1989)

Tadashi Suzuki mounted a rather eccentric 'postmodern' version of the play in Toga, Japan, which he deconstructed (together with *Three Sisters*) to form a production entitled *The Chekhov*. On a stage which looked like an abstract of a Kabuki-style setting, six actors played most of the roles each wearing 'a Groucho nose, spectacles, and mustache, black swallow-tailed jacket, lavender gloves, no shorts and no pants'. All held open umbrellas and crept, leapt or hobbled around the playing area inside 'oversized wicker panniers cut open at the bottom'. The style of vocal delivery was 'a barked, highly emphatic form' reminiscent of Noh theatre. 'At one startling moment amplified claps of sound seemed to devastate all the figures onstage: they recovered with tortured, spastic slowness, as though reacting to the dropping and after-effects of a nuclear bomb or of a Chernobyl-like disaster' (Albert Bermel, *Comic Agony: Mixed Impressions in the Modern Theatre*, Evanston, Ill., Northwestern University Press, 1993, pp.55–6).

At the Warsaw Studio Theatre, in 1993, Jerzy Grzegorzewski staged *Uncle Vanya* in a style which parodied that of the Moscow Art Theatre:

> The vast stage was cluttered with Chekhovian detritus – garden furniture, a grand piano, a tripod camera, a bench, white trunks of birches – cheek by jowl with the bare skeleton of an airplane wing and a white canvas daubed in grey. The indispensable samovar existed in several variants of different sizes, and was regularly disassembled and reassembled. For all the space, crucial scenes took place in a narrow passage between the stage and the first row or in labyrinthine corridors or almost in the wings [...] The play opened with Marina and Astrov in slow motion moving the samovar from one end of the table to another, endless pauses interrupting their 'game'. During Serebryakov's lecture, his auditors were seated back-to-back in straight chairs like a train to nowhere. [...] The goodbyes of Act IV were the occasion for a photograph, but no one actually left. As they made a show of departing, they took up seats in the passage like an auxiliary audience. (Senelick, 1997, pp.347–8)

The German director, Peter Stein, staged an Italian version of the play, at the Teatro Argentina, Rome, in 1996, which attracted widespread critical acclaim. The setting, by Ferdinand Wogerbauer, 'presented the changing scene with brilliant clarity as each act gives way to the next, [beginning] out of doors in the clearing of a birchwood, the whole surrounded by a frame [...] of bleached timbers: and as scene follows scene, this 'frame' slowly encroaches, additions transforming it into a succession of ever more busy interiors until, in the final scene claustrophobia is all but complete' (*Plays International*, November 1996, p.26). Peter Stein was staggered by the radical nature of the play and its use of a limited vocabulary, which he estimated at a mere thousand words, as well as by the power of its pauses and silences. Michael Billington was impressed, describing it as:

the tragedy of two women, united but separated by their fatal
passion for Astrov. [...] Elisabetta Pozzi lends [Sonya] a rapt
devotion and burning ecstasy that makes you aware Astrov is
turning down the chance of a lifetime. There is a heart-stopping
moment in the second act when their bodies brush and their lips
almost touch and you realise that Astrov – played by Remo Girone
with just the right mixture of sensitivity and coarseness – is simply
leaning past her to get a bottle of vodka. [...] Maddalena
Crippa's Elena is both her spiritual soul mate and physical
antithesis [...] In the scene where Astrov describes Russia's
deforestation she giggles inappropriately as he talks of 'flora' and
'fauna' and her hands hover about his neck as if yearning to hug
him [...] before they finally part, her hands caress Astrov's
travelling bag, his medical phials and even his pencil. [...]
Tragedy [...] unites with comedy in the great moment when
Vanya takes a pot-shot at the Professor and succeeds only in
puncturing a flower-vase: the very one containing the autumn roses
he has, in a gesture of supreme futility, offered to Elena. (*Guardian*,
17 April 1996)

A production by Barbara Frey, at the Munich Residenztheater,
2004, prompted comparison with a Scots dialect version by John
Byrne, *Uncle Varick*, and pointed to the sheer variety of translated
versions of the play on offer. Frey staged her *Onkel Wanya* as an
outright comedy, in a setting by Bettina Meier which consisted of:

A white box with a square aperture at the back and on each side.
Little flap-down seats built into the walls offered no comfort zone
for actors to flop into. This meant stand-up conversations, and
perched comic indignity for Serebryakov's self-pitying night scene.
The only props were a small table with a samovar, a selection of
vodka and wine, some papers and a bakelite Fifties radio which
was occasionally switched on, once comically, by a stray bullet
from Vanya's gun. The costumes too were Fifties, Vanya in a tank
top, Sonya in a pink twin-set [...] Astrov observed events with
amused, disillusioned detachment [...] Yelena [...] in a slinky
blue satin dress [...] could gently brush off [...] Vanya [...]
be an understanding confidante to Sonya or a Hollywood vamp to
Astrov. [...] The play was performed without interval, and the
act divisions were marked by full-stage projections of the family
walking in sun-drenched meadows. (Hugh Rorrison, *Plays
International*, July/August 2004, p.30)

Further Reading

Allen, David, *Performing Chekhov*, London, Routledge, 2000

Barricelli, Jean-Pierre (ed.), *Chekhov's Great Plays: A Critical Anthology*, New York and London, New York University Press, 1981

Bentley, Eric, *In Search of Theatre*, Alfred Knopf, New York, 1953, Vintage Books, New York, 1954

Chekhov, Anton, *The Wood Demon, Uncle Vanya*, trans. Ronald Hingley, in *The Oxford Chekhov*, vol. III, London and New York, OUP, 1964

Emeljanow, Victor (ed.), *Chekhov: The Critical Heritage*, London, Routledge & Kegan Paul, 1981

Gilman, Richard, *Chekhov's Plays: An Opening into Eternity*, New Haven and London, Yale University Press, 1995

Gottlieb, Vera and Allain, Paul (eds), *The Cambridge Companion to Chekhov*, Cambridge, CUP, 2000

Magarshack, David, *Chekhov the Dramatist*, London, John Lehmann, 1952; reissued London, Eyre Methuen, 1980

Miles, Patrick (ed.), *Chekhov on the British Stage*, Cambridge, CUP, 1993

Peace, Richard, *Chekhov: A Study of the Four Major Plays*, New Haven and London, Yale University Press, 1983

Pitcher, Harvey, *The Chekhov Play: A New Interpretation*, London, Chatto & Windus, 1973

Rayfield, Donald, *Chekhov's 'Uncle Vania' and 'The Wood Demon'*, London, Bristol Classical Press, 1995

Senelick, Laurence, *Anton Chekhov*, Basingstoke and London, Macmillan, 1985

Senelick, Laurence, *The Chekhov Theatre: A Century of the Plays in Performance*, Cambridge, CUP, 1997

Styan, J.L., *Chekhov in Performance: A Commentary on the Major Plays*, Cambridge, CUP, 1971

Tchekhov, Anton, *Oncle Vania*, (in French) trans. Tonia Galievsky and Bruno Sermonne, with commentary and notes by Patrice Pavis, Paris, Le Livre de Poche, 1986

Valency, Maurice, *The Breaking String: The Plays of Anton*

Chekhov, New York, OUP, 1966
Worrall, Nick, *File on Chekhov*, London, Methuen, 1986

Videos

Laurence Olivier's Production of 'Uncle Vanya', dir. Stuart Burge, a BHE Production in association with the Chichester Festival Theatre, London, 1962 (B&W, 120 mins)
Vanya on 42nd Street, André Gregory's production adapted by David Mamet, dir. Louis Malle, Mayfair Entertainment International/Channel 4, USA, 1994 (col., 115 mins)

Translator's Introduction

No one knows exactly when *Uncle Vanya* took its present form. It was most probably in 1896, between the completion of *The Seagull* in the spring of that year and its disastrous première in St Petersburg that October. It was first produced in the following year, as the second of Chekhov's four last great plays. But in its origins it goes back to a much earlier period than any of them. It is substantially a reworking of *The Wood Demon*, which was conceived nearly a decade before, when Chekhov was twenty-eight, and still only just emerging as a serious writer. Its development into its final form was tortuous and painful, and it is the story of Chekhov's own development as a dramatist. It was many times nearly abandoned; so was Chekhov's new career. At an early point both play and career nearly took off in a startlingly different direction, when Chekhov proposed changing the subject to the story in the Apocrypha of Holofernes and his decapitation by Judith, or else Solomon, or alternatively Napoleon on Elba, or Napoleon III and Eugénie. The possibilities are as extraordinary to consider as Vanya's own missed alternative career as a Schopenhauer or a Dostoyevsky.

Chekhov's original conception was bizarre enough. It was for a collaboration between himself and Suvorin, the wealthy publisher who was, somewhat improbably, his closest friend. Suvorin had literary ambitions of his own, and wrote stories which he submitted to Chekhov's practical and often devastating criticism, and a play, *Tatyana Repina*, which Chekhov parodied. The first work on the proposed collaboration seems in fact to have been done by Suvorin rather than Chekhov. In a letter written in November 1888 – the earliest reference to the joint venture – Chekhov acknowledges receipt of 'the beginning of the play', and congratulates Suvorin on the creation of one of the principal characters – Blagosvetlov, who was to become Serebryakov in the final version. 'You've done him well: he's tiresome and irritating from the very first words, and if the audience listens to him for three to five minutes at a stretch, precisely the right impression will be produced. The spectator will think: "Oh, dry up, do!" This person, i.e. Blagosvetlov, should have the effect on the spectator of both a clever, gouty, old grouser and a dull musical comedy which is going on for too long.' It was a little ironical that this tedious character was Suvorin's contribution to the enterprise, because some people thought later that Chekhov had *based* him on Suvorin.

In the same letter Chekhov goes on to remind Suvorin of 'the bill of our play' – a list of eleven characters, with a description of each of them. Of these eleven, four can be recognised as the precursors of characters in the final version of *Uncle Vanya*. One of them, Blagosvetlov's daughter, bears little resemblance to the plain, hard-working Sonya she eventually became, and is more like Yelena, her lethargic and beautiful stepmother. But the other three are already the substantial originals of Serebryakov, Astrov, and Vanya himself. Blagosvetlov is a retired government official, not an academic, but he is 'of clerical origins, and was educated in a seminary. The position he occupied was achieved through his own efforts . . . Suffers from gout, rheumatism, insomnia, and tinnitus. His landed property he got as a dowry . . . Can't abide mystics, visionaries, holy fools, poets, or pious Peters, doesn't believe in God, and is accustomed to regard the entire world from the standpoint of practical affairs. Practical affairs first, last, and foremost, and everything else – nonsense or humbug.' Astrov, at this stage, is still a landowner rather than a doctor. But he already has his amazingly prescient concern for the ecology (and is already nicknamed the Wood Demon because of it). He already believes that 'the forests create the climate, the climate influences the character of the people, etc., etc. There is neither civilisation nor happiness if the forests are ringing under the axe, if the climate is harsh and cruel, if people are harsh and cruel as well . . . ' Blagosvetlov's daughter is attracted to him, as Yelena is in *Vanya*, 'not for his ideas, which are alien to her, but for his talent, for his passion, for his wide horizons . . . She likes the way his brain has swept over the whole of Russia and over ten centuries ahead . . . '

His account of the proto-Vanya is brief, and contains characteristics which are later discarded ('Drinks Vichy water and grouses away. Behaves arrogantly. Stresses that he is not frightened of generals. Shouts'). But in outline Uncle Vanya is already there – and in describing him Chekhov is also laying down the first outline of the plot: 'The brother of Blagosvetlov's late wife. Manages Blagosvetlov's estate (his own he has long since run through). Regrets he has not stolen. He had not foreseen that his Petersburg relations would have such a poor appreciation of his services. They don't understand him – they don't want to understand him – and he regrets he has not stolen.'

Chekhov says in his letter he will sketch out the rest of Act One himself and send it to Suvorin. He undertakes not to touch Blagosvetlov, and suggests sharing the work on Blagosvetlov's daughter, because 'I'll never be able to manage her on my own'. The great arborealist will be Chekhov's up to Act Four, then Suvorin's up to a certain scene where Chekhov will take over because Suvorin will never manage to catch the right tone of voice. Then he will leave Suvorin to start Act Two, as he did Act One.

It is difficult to believe that this strange two-headed beast would have been any substitute for the *Vanya* it would presumably have displaced. Fortunately, perhaps, Suvorin seems to have backed down, and left Blagosvetlov as his sole contribution, because a month later Chekhov was writing to ask him why he was refusing to collaborate on *The Wood Demon* (as it was by this time called), and offering to find a new subject altogether if Suvorin would prefer it. This was when he proposed switching to Holofernes or Solomon, or one of the two Napoleans.[1] But not

---

[1] Chekhov himself did in fact start on the Solomon project, and the following fragment was found among his papers. The metaphysical anguish which the king expresses in this monologue appears to derive not from the figure of wealth and wisdom in Chronicles but from the author of Ecclesiastes. The ascription to Solomon in the first verse of Ecclesiastes ('The words of the Preacher, the son of David, king in Jerusalem') was once taken literally, but is now thought to be conventional. The book is now considered to be the work of a much later author, and its wonderful melancholy Epicurean charm more Hellenistic than Judaic.

SOLOMON (*alone*). O, how dark life is! No night in all its blackness when I was a child struck such terror into me as does my unfathomed existence. My God, to my father David Thou gavest but the gift of bringing words and sounds together as one, of singing and praising Thee with plucked strings, of sweetly weeping, of wresting tears from the eyes of others and of finding favour with beauty; but to me why gavest Thou also a languishing spirit and unsleeping hungry thought? Like an insect born out of the dust I hide in darkness, and trembling, chilled, despairing, fearful, see and hear in all things a fathomless mystery. To what end does this light of morning serve? To what end does the sun rise from behind the Temple and gild the palm-tree? To what end is the beauty of women? Whither is yonder bird hastening, what is the meaning of its flight, if it and its fledglings and the place to which it

even the attractions of a biblical or historical subject could tempt the literary-minded magnate back into harness, and the following spring Chekhov reluctantly began to struggle with the material on his own.

There were some moments of elation in the weeks that followed, judging at any rate from the bulletins to Suvorin. 'Act Three is so scandalous that when you see it you'll say: "This was written by a cunning and pitiless man" ... ', 'The play is terribly strange, and I'm surprised that such strange things are emerging from my pen.' There were also more or less simultaneous moments of discouragement, when he informed other correspondents that he was not going to write plays, and that he was not attracted by the idea of fame as a dramatist. By the end of May, with only two acts written, he had given up, and in September he had to start all over again from the beginning.

Then, when it was at last finished, the play was rejected out of hand by both the Alexandrinsky Theatre in St Petersburg, which had just successfully staged *Ivanov*, and by the Maly in Moscow. An unofficial meeting of the Petersburg section of the Theatrical-Literary Committee, which vetted all the plays submitted for production in the imperial theatres, judged it 'a fine dramatised story, but not a drama'. Lensky, the actor for whose benefit performance the play had been offered to the Maly, returned the manuscript to Chekhov with a particularly crushing dismissal. 'I will say only one thing: write a story. You are too contemptuous of the stage and of the dramatic form, you have too little respect for them, to write drama. This form is harder than that of the story, and you – forgive me – are too spoiled by success to study as it were the basic ABC of the dramatic form, and to learn to love it.' Even Nemirovich-Danchenko, another member of the committee, who was later of course to be a co-founder with Stanislavsky of the Moscow Art Theatre and one of Chekhov's most important patrons, thought that Lensky was right in diagnosing ignorance of the demands of the stage (though he

---

hurries must come like me to dust? Oh, better I had never been born, or that I were a stone to which God had given neither eyes nor thoughts. To weary my body for the night I yesterday like a common workman dragged marble to the Temple; now the night is come, and I cannot sleep ... I will go and lie down again ... Forses used to tell me that if one imagines a flock of sheep running and thinks hard about it then one's thoughts will dissolve and sleep. This will I do ... (*Exit.*)

thought Chekhov could easily master them). 'Say what you like,' he wrote, 'clear, lifelike characters, an interesting conflict, and the proper development of the plot – these are the best guarantee of success on the stage. A play cannot succeed without a plot, but the most serious fault is lack of clarity, when the audience can't possibly grasp the essence of the plot. This is more important than any stage tricks or effects.' Chekhov swore again – not for the last time – to give up playwriting. But in the end he rewrote once more, and did a completely new version of the last act, with which he had been having difficulties from the beginning. The play was then produced, in December 1889, by a Moscow commercial management. It was dismissed by the critics not only as untheatrical, but also as 'a blind transcription of everyday reality', and was taken off after three performances.

With hindsight, the most remarkable thing about *The Wood Demon* is how much of *Uncle Vanya* is already there – often word for word. All the essential material of Act One, including most of the big speeches; almost the whole of Act Two; and in Act Three the entire scene in which Serebryakov proposes to sell the estate. It seems amazing that this wealth of brilliant scenes was not enough to alert even the most sluggish producer and the most jaded critic to Chekhov's powers in the theatre. But it is true that they fail to make the impact they should because he had not yet overcome certain faults recognisable from his two earlier full-length plays, *Ivanov* and the one written when he was a student (untitled, but called *Platonov* in some versions and *Wild Honey* in mine). The characters are too simple; too noble and Tolstoyan in the case of Orlovsky, the debauched son of a local landowner. The setting of the first and last acts has wandered in pursuit of the picturesque; and there is something unsettling about the tone of the whole. It may have seemed offensively naturalistic to contemporary critics, but to the modern reader it veers more towards the facetiousness of Chekhov's early comic journalism, and towards a certain bucolic jollity, which sit oddly with the story that is beginning to emerge. At the end of Act Three all resemblance to the later version ceases. Vanya attempts to shoot not Serebryakov but himself, and succeeds. So the last act is left without a Vanya, and instead proceeds by way of a sunset picnic alongside an old watermill to a happy ending, with the Serebryakovs more to less reconciled, the Wood Demon and Sonya paired off, and even the debauched Orlovsky settling down with a nice girl. Nemirovich-

Danchenko's assessment of the play is shrewd; the story is not clear. And the reason is that Chekhov has not yet recognised the story he is trying to tell.

After its failure in Moscow the play was abandoned again, and might well have remained so for good. It seems to have been Prince Urusov, a jurist and well-known literary figure, who provoked Chekhov into starting work on it again – somewhat ironically, because Urusov admired the earlier version so much that he persisted to the end in believing that Chekhov had ruined it by turning it into *Uncle Vanya*. It was Urusov's request for permission to reprint the text of *The Wood Demon*, in fact, that made Chekhov re-read it. He evidently did not like what he saw (years later he was still telling the loyal Urusov: 'I hate that play and I try to forget about it') and it was presumably this reawakened dissatisfaction that made him set to work on it again. The internal evidence, at any rate – the dates of the diaries and notebooks which were the provenance of some of the material in the new version – suggests that the reworking was done the following year, in 1896; and in a letter to Suvorin written that December is the first reference to *Uncle Vanya* – already, apparently, a finished text. If this dating is correct then the project was probably only just completed in time, because after the débâcle with the St Petersburg opening of *The Seagull* in October he once again swore off playwriting.

The play in its new form still faced one final rebuff. The Maly Theatre asked for it, which gave the Theatrical-Literary Committee the chance to produce an even more magisterial rejection and scheme of improvement than before. Its report identified a number of 'unevennesses or lacunae' in the play, and complained of 'longueurs', such as 'the extended eulogy of forests, shared between Sonya and Astrov, and the explanation of Astrov's theory of arboriculture'. The committee was worried about the distressing frequency with which it believed Vanya and Astrov were shown suffering from hangovers, and the unfortunate effect that would be produced if this were thought to be the cause of Vanya's attempt to shoot Serebryakov. It felt that Vanya and Astrov 'as it were merge into a single type of failure, of superfluous man', and it complained that 'nothing prepares us for the powerful outburst of passion which occurs during the conversation with Yelena'. It reserved its greatest concern, though, for Vanya's treatment of Serebryakov. 'That Vanya could take a dislike to the professor as

Yelena's husband is understandable,' it conceded; 'that his
sermonising and moralising cause irritation is also natural, but the
disillusionment with Serebryakov's academic stature, and indeed
more precisely with him as an art historian, is somewhat strange
... nor is it a reason for his being pursued with pistol shots, for
his being hunted down by someone who is no longer responsible
for his actions.' The unfairness of shooting professors because you
have a low opinion of their academic achievements seems to have
spoken deeply to the committee's learned members.

This time, however, Chekhov declined all suggestions for
rewriting. By now, in any case, the play had been successfully
produced in a number of provincial theatres, and it was finally
established in Moscow by being produced at the Art Theatre –
though its reception there was initially more muted than the
hysterical success which *The Seagull* had just enjoyed in the same
place. With hindsight we can see that Chekhov's reworking of the
material from *The Wood Demon*, whenever it was done, has
shifted it across the crucial divide that separates the four last plays
from all his earlier ones – from all the earlier ones in the world.

Some of the changes he has made are straightforward
improvements in dramatic technique. He has concentrated the
setting of the play on the place where the real events of the story
actually happen – the Serebryakovs' estate – and he has stripped
out the superfluous characters. But in the course of doing this he
has had an idea of genius. He has elided the debauched young
neighbour, Orlovsky, with the Wood Demon. The most upright
and selfless character in the original play is now the one who also
indulges in periodic drinking bouts; instead of being in love with
Sonya he is now, like Orlovsky, first coarsely knowing about
Vanya's relations with Yelena, and then ready to propose a
passing liaison with her himself; he has become Astrov in all his
dark, self-contained complexity. And Yelena, a figure of
uncompromised virtue in the original version, has become
fascinated by him, so that, engaged as she is to advance poor
Sonya's cause with him, she has become touched by the same
characteristic ambiguity.

With these changes the whole tone of the play has been
modified. The bucolic geniality and the facetiousness have gone,
and left exposed the sense of wasted life at the heart of the story.
By the same token the mood has changed from one of comfortable
idleness to one of uncomfortably interrupted work. The importance

of work in these last four plays is not always grasped. An impression lingers that they are about impoverished gentry with nothing to do all day but watch their fortunes decline; 'Chekhovian' is a synonym for a sort of genteel, decaying, straw-hatted ineffectualness. There are such characters, it's true – Telegin, the ruined neighbour who is living on Vanya's charity, Gayev and his sister in *The Cherry Orchard* – but they are few in number. Why do we tend to pick on them when we think about these harsh plays? A bizarre combination of nostalgia and condescension, perhaps – nostalgia for a lost world of servants and rural leisure, easy condescension from the moral superiority of our own busy lives. What we forget, when we are not face to face with them, is that most of the people in these plays are not members of the leisured class at all. They have to earn their living, and earn it through hard professional work. We catch them at moments of leisure, because this is when they can stand back and look at their lives, but their thoughts are with their jobs. The memory that remains with us from *The Seagull* is of people sitting in a garden and enjoying their 'sweet country boredom'. Who are these idle folk? They are two actresses, two writers, a doctor, a teacher, a civil servant, and a hard-pressed estate manager. Some of them have time to sit down because they are only at the beginning of their careers, some because they are at the end; the others are simply on holiday. The idleness of Masha and Andrey, in *Three Sisters*, is remarkable because it is in such contrast to the drudgery of Masha's husband and her other two sisters; the idleness of the fading landowners in *The Cherry Orchard* is being swept aside by the industrious energy of the new entrepreneurs and activists. At the centre of *Vanya* is a woman so drugged with idleness that she can't walk straight; but the corrupting effects of this are felt in the lives around her, and they are lives of hitherto unceasing toil – whether the pedantic labours of her husband, or the agricultural stewardship of Vanya and Sonya, or the sleepless rural medicine of Astrov. These working lives are already the background of *The Wood Demon*, but there they remain offstage, somewhat secondary to the picnicking and moralising. In the final version, Vanya's bitterness over his years of misdirected sacrifice has become the centre of the action, and its culmination is now the resumption by Vanya and Sonya of their labours. In fact they resume them on stage, in front of our eyes. This is not the first time that work has been shown on stage. In *The Weavers*, first

produced in Berlin three years earlier, Hauptmann had shown the
wretched weavers labouring at their looms. For that matter we see
the gravediggers briefly at work in *Hamlet*, and we have seen
plenty of servants serving, soldiers soldiering, and actors
rehearsing. But this is surely the first great theatrical classic where
we see the principals set about the ordinary, humdrum business of
their lives. In fact work is one of the central themes in Chekhov.
Work as the longed-for panacea for all the ills of idleness; work as
obsession and drudgery and the destruction of life; work as life,
simply. What Sonya looks forward to in heaven for herself and her
uncle at the end of the present play is not finding peace, as some
translations have it; what she says, five times over, in plain
everyday Russian, is that they will *rest*.

Chekhov's second masterstroke in the rewriting, even more
fundamental and consequential than the new ambiguity of the
characters, is his alteration to the aim of Vanya's revolver. All his
full-length plays up to this point have resolved with the death of
one of the central characters. Now, instead of letting Vanya
likewise tidy himself away after his confrontation with
Serebryakov, he has had the idea of making him turn murderer
instead of suicide – and of failing.

In the first place this is simply a more interesting development.
For the pacific and long-suffering Vanya to have been driven to
attempt murder tells us much more about the intensity of his anger
and of his sense of betrayal; and his missing the target is
something he at once recognises as bitterly characteristic. This is
slightly obscured by the traditional translation of his line. 'Missed
again!' sounds as if it refers only to the two shots. The word he
uses in Russian, however, refers not only to a missed shot but to
any kind of mistake (see A Note on the Translation). What he is
thinking of is surely all the missed opportunities in his life, and in
particular his failure to have made advances to Yelena when she
was still free. Then again, the fact that he misses at point-blank
range opens up a whole series of questions about the nature of
these mistakes. Perhaps they are not serious attempts at all; even
as he pulls the trigger he *says* 'bang!', like a child with a toy
revolver. And even if he sees them as seriously intended, are they
examples of what a modern psychiatrist would call self-sabotage?
And if they are, is the unconscious objective to protect himself
from the consequences of success? Not only from being tried for
murder, but from being tested as a lover and husband, from

having the chance (as he at one moment believes he could have done if only he had lived 'normally') to become a Schopenhauer or a Dostoyevsky – and *then* failing, with no possibility of concealing his own responsibility for it?

In the second place, the failure of this dramatic gesture to have dramatic consequences destroys the drama; or rather it destroys the neatness with which the slow and confused changes of the world we inhabit are concentrated theatrically in simple and decisive events. The world of *Vanya* is the ambiguous and unresolved world of *The Seagull* – stripped of even the final note of resolution suggested by Konstantin's suicide. Most of the relatively few notes Chekhov gave to the director and actors were to do with this dislocation and diffusion. He missed the production in Moscow, because he had been exiled to Yalta for his consumption, but when he saw the play, on a tour the Art Theatre made in 1900 to the Crimea, one of the actresses in the company remembered his telling them afterwards that Sonya shouldn't kneel and kiss her father's hand on the line 'You must be merciful, father' at the end of Act Three, because 'after all that wasn't the drama. All the sense and all the drama of a person is on the inside, and not in external appearances. There was drama in Sonya's life up to this moment, there will be drama afterwards – but this is simply something that happens, a continuation of the shot. And the shot, in fact, is not drama – just something that happens.'[1] In a similar spirit he deprecated Stanislavsky's direction that Astrov should make his pass at Yelena, in Act Four, 'like a drowning man clutching at a straw'. By then, says Chekhov in a letter to Olga Knipper, who was playing Yelena, Astrov knows that nothing is going to come of his attraction to her, 'and he talks to her in this scene in the same tone of voice as he does about the heat in Africa, and kisses her in the most ordinary way, quite idly'. Stanislavsky remembered him as saying, after the performance in the Crimea, '"He kisses her like that, though." – And here he planted a brief kiss on his own hand. – "Astrov has no respect for Yelena. In fact when he leaves the house afterwards he's whistling."'

[1] There is something askew – and perhaps this is in keeping with the obliqueness of the play – about either Chekhov's note or the actress's memory of it, because his own stage direction calls for Sonya to kneel, if not to kiss her father's hand, while the line can hardly be construed as a 'continuation of the shot' because it occurs before it.

More important even than the nature of the failed murder are the consequences it has for the last act. Chekhov, as we have seen, had already tried various versions of this. What had caused the problem was his odd insistence, in all the variants of *The Wood Demon*, on placing Vanya's suicide at the end of Act Three, so that this traditional dramatic resolution still left everything unresolved for everyone else. But he had been feeling his way towards *something* with this arrangement, and now that Vanya remains alive it becomes clear what it is: precisely that – remaining alive. It is survival itself, the problem of going on with life *after* it has been robbed of hope and meaning. 'The ability to endure' had already been identified by Nina at the end of *The Seagull* as the most important quality in life. Now Sonya takes it up as her watchword – 'Endure, uncle! Endure!' – as she coaxes Vanya through his despair at the prospect of living for another dozen years, and as the future dwindles to a 'long, long succession of days and endless evenings' unilluminated by either any sense of purpose or any prospect of alteration. From now on the tragedy in Chekhov's plays will be not death but the continuance of life; the pain of losing the past, with all the happiness and wealth of possibilities it contained, will always be compounded by the pain of facing the future in all its emptiness. Two more characters will die, it is true. Tusenbach's death in *Three Sisters*, though, is shown not as *his* tragedy – the imminence of it gives him his first real awareness of the world and his first real pleasure in it – but as one more of the losses which empty the sisters' future of meaning. Firs is left dying at the end of *The Cherry Orchard*, but the sale of the estate, which finally destroys any hopes the Gayevs have had in life, has already occurred, like the attempted murder of Serebryakov, at the end of Act Three, so that the last act is left once again to show life continuing, and Gayev and his sister facing – with in this case what one might think to be an ironically misplaced insouciance – even grimmer futures still.

The insistence upon endurance is connected with another idea which first emerges in *Vanya*, and which will dominate *Three Sisters* as well – the conviction felt by some of the characters that the sufferings which stretch to the visible horizon of the future are in some way to be redeemed by a happiness lying beyond that horizon. Some of this optimism plainly has a quality of desperation about it; it is easy to recognise the obsessiveness with which Vershinin keeps returning to the idea that life on earth will be

'astonishingly, unimaginably beautiful' in two or three hundred
years' time, or perhaps a thousand, particularly since it doesn't
seem to matter to him exactly when, provided only the prospect
exists. But the two passionate and heartbreaking speeches with
which these plays end, by Sonya in the present play and by Olga
in *Three Sisters*, are something else again. The forms of
redemption that the two women expect are different; Sonya sees it
as coming only in the next world, but does see it as some kind of
personal recompense to herself and her uncle. Olga expects the
sufferings of the present to purchase happiness in this world – but
a happiness which will be experienced only 'by those who live
after us'. Both speeches, though, are so eloquent, and so
powerfully placed, that we cannot help wondering whether they
reflect some deep beliefs of this nature in Chekhov himself.

The external evidence in favour of this reading is slight. In his
notebooks he once expressed the hope that 'Man will become
better when we have shown him to himself as he is', and the
writer Vladimir Tikhonov remembered him as saying that once
people had seen themselves as they were 'they will surely by
themselves create a different and better life. I shall not see it, but I
know that everything will be changed, that nothing will be like
our present existence.' There is an echo of Vershinin here, if
Tikhonov has quoted him correctly, but it is a rare one. His notes
make it clear that the only unconditional prediction he made for
the future was that people would continue to think the past was
better. He had no utopian political views of any sort, as his
famous letter to another writer, Aleksei Pleshcheyev, makes clear.
In a letter to a third writer, Shcheglov, he states categorically that
he had no religion, which would rule out any possibility of his
entertaining the sort of hopes that Sonya does. And on a number
of occasions he specifically dissociated himself from the ideas of
his characters. 'If you're served coffee,' he says in a letter to
Suvorin, 'then don't try looking for beer in it. If I present you
with a professor's thoughts, then trust me and don't look for
Chekhov's thoughts in them.' For him as author, he says in the
same letter, his characters' ideas 'have no value for their content.
It's not a question of their content; that's changeable and it's not
new. The whole point is the nature of these opinions, their
dependence upon external influences and so on. They must be
examined like objects, like symptoms, entirely objectively, not
attempting either to agree with them or to dispute them. If I

described St Vitus' dance you wouldn't look at it from the point of view of a choreographer, would you? No? Then don't do it with opinions.' In another letter to Suvorin he took up the latter's complaint that one of his stories had not resolved the question of pessimism. 'I think that it's not for novelists to resolve such questions as God, pessimism, etc. The novelist's job is to show merely who, how, and in what circumstances people were talking or thinking about God or pessimism. The artist must be not the judge of his characters and what they are talking about, but merely an impartial witness. I heard a confused conversation, resolving nothing, between two Russian people about pessimism, and I have to pass on this conversation in the same form in which I heard it, but it will be evaluated by the jury, i.e. the readers. My job is merely to be talented, i.e. to be able to distinguish important phenomena from unimportant, to be able to illuminate characters and speak with their tongue.'

We do not have to suppose the author shares the beliefs expressed in these two speeches to find them moving, any more than we have to share the beliefs ourselves. The very remoteness, the very impossibility, of that sky dressed in diamonds, of that peace and happiness on earth, is what makes the speeches so poignant. And yet the force and insistence of the idea, in the two successive plays, is very striking. Even if they do not express beliefs which Chekhov shared, they may reveal a similarly poignant yearning of his own for a future whose unattainability he was just beginning to grasp. It is a common experience for people in early middle age, which is where Chekhov was when he wrote these plays, to come over the brow of the hill, as it were, and to see for the first time that their life will have an end. But the end with which Chekhov came face to face in mid-life was suddenly much closer still. It was not until six months after he had finished *Vanya* that he had his first major haemorrhage, and that his tuberculosis was finally diagnosed. But he had been spitting blood for a long time. He insists over and over again in his letters that this is the most normal thing in the world; but the more he insists the more one wonders. As Ronald Hingley puts it in his biography: 'Can Anton really have been unaware, still, that he suffered from tuberculosis? It seems incredible that a practising doctor could continue to ignore symptoms of which the possible purport might have struck any layman. On the other hand, as Chekhov's own works richly illustrate, human beings have an almost infinite capacity for self-deception. Did the man who deluded others about the desperate condition of his health also delude himself? Or did he hover between self-deception and self-knowledge?'

It was at some point in that final year before the diagnosis was made that he was writing *Vanya* in its definitive form and giving up the idea of death as a dramatic resolution. Perhaps somewhere inside himself he had begun to recognise what was happening to him. Perhaps, now that he was suddenly so close to it, death seemed a little less neat, a little less of an answer to the equation; perhaps it began to seem more like something you could look as far as, or beyond, but not at. And even if Chekhov hadn't yet seen the truth about his condition, perhaps Sonya and the others had in a sense seen it for him. A writer's characters, particularly when they are not forced to represent his conscious thoughts, can be appallingly well-informed about his unconscious ones. It is ironical. Chekhov most sedulously absented himself from his works. Sonya's passionate invocation of an afterlife in which he didn't believe may be one of our rare glimpses of him – and of an aspect of him that he couldn't even see himself.

MICHAEL FRAYN

A Note on the Translation

I have extended my usual ruthlessness with Russian personal names to the French variants of them which are occasionally used in the original of this play. 'Hélène' is too remote from 'Yelena' for English ears to make the connection fast enough. I have, however, retained Maria Vasilyevna's 'Alexandre' for 'Aleksandr' (indistinguishable when written in the Cyrillic, and only marginally distinguishable when spoken) and her 'Jean' for Vanya, which do seem in some way characteristic of her abstraction from the muddy realities of Russian rural life.

There are as usual one or two literary allusions in the text. The Ostrovsky play that Astrov refers to in Act One, when he is looking for his cap to leave, is *The Girl Without a Dowry*. Paratov, the reckless, dashing cad who has broken the heart of the girl in the title, and who is just about to break it again, introduces himself to Karandyshev, her pusillanimous fiancé, in the words that Astrov quotes – 'a man with large moustaches and small abilities'. Astrov has presumably prompted himself to think of Ostrovsky by what he has muttered just before this, which is a quotation from a character in another of Ostrovsky's plays, *Wolves and Sheep*. In its original context it is an incoherent protestation of ignorance from a timid aunt when she is interrogated by the despotic local matriarch about whether her niece already has a suitor. The point of the line in its original context is its comical incoherence, but out of that context it is so elliptical as to be meaningless, and I have cut it. Astrov is quoting again in Act Two when he talks to Sonya about Yelena's beauty. The line comes from Pushkin's poem, *The Tale of the Dead Princess and the Seven Bogatyrs*. This is the same story as *Snow White and the Seven Dwarfs* (though the *bogatyrs* with whom Pushkin's princess finds refuge are not dwarfs but the warrior-heroes of Russian folk-tales), and the line is adapted from what the mirror says to the wicked stepmother after she has disposed of her rival. To make this clear I have modified it to refer to its more familiar equivalent in Grimm. There is plainly an ironical parallel between the mirror's telling the stepmother about the stepdaughter's beauty, and Astrov's telling the stepdaughter about the stepmother's beauty.

There is another literary reference which I have cut, as having no point but its familiarity, and no familiarity in translation (probably none today even in Russia). When Vanya in Act One describes Serebryakov writing in his study from morning until far into the night he adds in the original a quotation from a satire upon odes by one I.I. Dmitriev (1760–1837), which in translation would run roughly:

> We rack our brains and crease our brow,
> And scribble odes and more odes yet.
> But not the smallest hint of praise.
> Do either odes or author get.

I have also, for similar reasons, cut the words of the song that Astrov sings in the middle of the night, in Act Two, and his reference, later in the same scene, to his *Feldscher's* idiosyncratic pronunciation. I have made a slight change in the wonderful scene in the same act where Yelena and Sonya are reconciled. What they do in the original is drink *Bruderschaft*, and what they thereby resolve to be to each in future, of course, is *ty*, the second person singular. I have made another small change in Act Four, when Telegin in the original describes Vanya's attempt to shoot Serebryakov as 'a subject worthy of Aivazovsky's brush'. Aivazovsky was a nineteenth-century painter who was most celebrated for his marine studies, though he also painted a number of battle scenes, and it may be these that Telegin had in mind. He produced some six thousand works, but not even this impressive productivity will make his name meaningful to a modern English audience.

I regret any pain caused by the demolition of two landmarks familiar to generations of English audiences. 'Missed again!' or something like it is a funnier line than Chekhov's, but fails to capture an important part of the sense. What Vanya says in the original is 'A *promakh* again?!' A *promakh* is not just a miss; it is any kind of mistake or false move, and surely (see p. lxxix) refers to more than just the two shots. Then there is the question of Telegin's nickname. This is given in every translation I have come across as 'Waffles'. The Russian, *Vaflya*, does indeed mean a waffle, but Telegin is given the name, as he explains, because of his pockmarked appearance. I can find no grounds for believing that 'Waffles' suggests the after-effects of smallpox. It sounds comfortably like an English nickname, it is true, but its implications are surely all wrong. To modern English ears it might indicate a taste for meaningless verbiage; nearer the time, according to Partridge, a waffles (low, 1904) was 'a loafer, a sauntering idler'. Telegin's speech becomes confused when he is upset, but he doesn't waffle. He is idle, certainly, but his idleness is not sauntering – it goes with his abnegation, humility, and saintly devotion to the ideals of love and marriage. I can think of no English nickname that suggests pockmarks. And even if a suitable English equivalent did exist, there would surely be something odd about applying it to a Russian. A lot of English nicknames sound embarrassing enough attached to Englishmen; applied to Russians, nursery locutions such as 'Waffles', 'Boofy', 'Bingo', etc. seem as bogus as spats and co-respondent shoes. It is like the curious practice which is followed in some English versions of Chekhov's plays of translating Russian given names. Never 'Vanya', for some reason – I know of no translation entitled *Uncle Jack* – but Ronald Hingley gives 'Helen Serebryakov' and 'Michael Astrov'. Why should Russians be the only people to enjoy the advantage of anglicisation? Why not Charles Marx and Henry Ibsen? John-James Rousseau and Leonard from Vinci? The only possible proceeding with '*Vaflya*', it seemed to me in the end, was to leave it out. I have made do with the occasional diminutive, and shifted Telegin's reference to his pockmarks into his earlier remarks about his 'unprepossessing appearance'.

One idea I have stolen from Hingley, however. In the original, Serebryakov is planning to use the money left over from the sale of the estate to buy a modest dacha 'in Finland'. Finland was at the time, of course, a grand duchy of the Russian Empire, but it seems at first sight mysterious why Serebryakov should want to live in the countryside there if he can't stand the countryside anywhere else in Russia. Its attraction, though, as Hingley's phrase makes clear, was no doubt that the Finnish frontier was only twenty miles from St Petersburg.

In Act Two, according to the stage direction, 'the watchman can be heard knocking in the garden'. The knocking was to warn off intruders, and it was traditionally done with a *kolotushka* – a kind of mallet – against a piece of wood.

Finally, a very hesitant gloss of a line which I have left as opaque as it is in the original. It comes in the scene where Astrov is telling Sonya that there is no light in the distance for him because there is no one he loves. In describing his life he says that he is 'ceaselessly pummelled by fate'. He offers no details, and to English ears it sounds the kind of thing that Russians tend to say in plays. Sometimes, however, they say things like this with very specific meaning. The phrase recalls Ranyevskaya's complaint to Trofimov, the 'Wandering Student' in *The Cherry Orchard*, that 'you do nothing but get yourself tossed by fate from one place to the next' – and we know from one of Chekhov's letters what *this* manifestation of fate was. Trofimov is 'perpetually being exiled, perpetually being thrown out of the university' for his political activities, and there is no way in which Chekhov can get a direct reference to this past the censorship. Does Astrov have similar views and similar problems? I know of no external evidence to support this interpretation, but one has always to be prepared for the lines between the lines in Russian texts. I once translated a play by a Soviet writer in which a character said of his grandfather simply that he had 'recently returned to Moscow'. I remember how foolishly over-suspicious I felt when I asked the author if the absence of any reference to where he had returned *from* could possibly imply that it had been exile, or the camps. I also remember how naive I felt when I saw his surprise that I should have to ask, since it was already there in black and white, as he saw it, clearly stated in good plain Russian.

M.F.

The Pronunciation of the Names

The following is an approximate practical guide. In general, all stressed 'a's are pronounced as in 'far' (the sound is indicated below by 'aa') and all stressed 'o's as in 'more' (they are written below as 'aw'). All unstressed 'a's and 'o's are thrown away and slurred. The 'u's are pronounced as in 'crude'; they are shown below as 'oo'. A 'y' at the beginning of a syllable, in front of another vowel, is pronounced as a consonant (i.e. as in 'yellow', not as in 'sky').

The characters:

Se-re-brya-*kawf*
Yel*ya*yna
*Saw*nya
Ma*ree*ya Va*seel*yevna
*Vaan*ya
*Aa*strov
Tel*ya*ygin (Eel*ya* Eel*yeech* – Eel*yoosh*a)
Ma*reen*a

Other names occurring in the play, in alphabetical order:

Batyushkov – *Baat*yooskhov
Dostoyevsky – Dosto*yev*sky
Ivan Ivanich – Ee*vaan* Ee*vaan*ich
Kharkov – *Khaar*kov
Kursk – Koorsk
Malitzkoye – *Maal*-itz-ko-ye
Mama – *Maam*a
Papa – *Paap*a
Pavel Alekseyevich – *Paav*el Alek*say*evich
Turgenev – Toor-*gain*-yev
Yefim – Ye*feem*

Uncle Vanya

This translation of *Uncle Vanya* was first produced by Michael Codron at the Vaudeville Theatre, London, on 24 May 1988, with the following cast:

SEREBRYAKOV, *professor emeritus*	Benjamin Whitrow
YELENA, *his wife, twenty-seven*	Greta Scacchi
SONYA, *his daughter by his first marriage*	Imelda Staunton
MARIA VASILYEVNA, *the widowed mother of the professor's first wife*	Rachel Kempson
VANYA, *her son*	Michael Gambon
ASTROV, *a doctor*	Jonathan Pryce
TELEGIN, *an impoverished landowner*	Jonathan Cecil
MARINA, *the old nurse*	Elizabeth Bradley
WORKMAN	Tom Hardy
WATCHMAN	Peter Honri

Directed by Michael Blakemore
Designed by Tanya McCallin
Lighting by Mick Hughes
Associate Producer David Sutton

The action takes place on Professor Serebryakov's estate.

Act One

The garden, with part of the house, and the verandah. On the path, beneath an ancient poplar, stands a table set with tea-things. Garden seats and chairs; on one of the seats lies a guitar. Near the table is a swing. Early afternoon. Overcast.

MARINA, a dumpy old woman who moves only with difficulty, is sitting by the samovar and knitting a stocking. ASTROV is walking up and down nearby.

MARINA (*pours a glass of tea*). Here you are, then, my dear.

ASTROV (*takes the glass reluctantly*). I don't really want it.

MARINA. A drop of vodka, perhaps?

ASTROV. No. I don't drink vodka every day. It's too close, for that matter. (*Pause.*) Nanna, how long have we known each other?

MARINA (*thinking about it*). How long? Oh my Lord, I wish I could remember ... You arrived in these parts ... when ...? Sonya's mother was still alive. Her last two winters you were coming to us ... So that's, what, eleven years. (*After a moment's thought.*) Or maybe even longer ...

ASTROV. I've changed a lot in that time?

MARINA. Oh, a lot. You were a young man then, you were good-looking. You've aged, my love. Your looks aren't what they were. And then you like your drop to drink.

ASTROV. Yes ... In the last ten years I've become a different man. You know why, Nanna? Because I've had to work too hard. On my feet from morning to night – never a moment to myself – go to bed and lie there just waiting to be dragged out again to a patient. In all the time we've known each other I've had not a single day off. Of course I've aged. Anyway, life is a dull, stupid, dirty business at the best of times. It drags its feet, this life of ours. You're surrounded by cranks and crackbrains – there's something odd about the lot of them. Live with them for a few years and gradually, without noticing it, you start getting a bit odd yourself. It's inevitable. (*Twirling his long moustache.*) Look, I've grown this great moustache. Stupid thing. I've got a bit odd, Nanna ... I haven't gone soft in the head yet, thank God, my brains are all there, only my feelings have got somehow blunted. Nothing I want. Nothing I need. No one I love ... Just you, maybe. (*Kisses her head.*) I had a nanny like you when I was a child.

MARINA. You want something to eat, perhaps?

ASTROV. No. In the third week of Lent I went over to Malitzkoye – they had an epidemic there ... Typhus ... Peasants lying packed together in their huts ... Mud, stench, calves on the floor alongside the patients ... Baby pigs, even ... I was on the go all day, not a moment to sit down, nothing to eat or drink ... Got home, and still no chance to rest because they'd carted a shunter in from the railway. I put him on the table to operate, and he goes and dies on me under the chloroform. And just when I didn't need them my feelings came to life, and I got a stab of conscience as if I'd killed him deliberately ... I sat down and I closed my eyes, so, and I thought: the people who come after us, a hundred, two hundred years from now, the people we're beating a path for – will they ever spare a thought for us? They won't, Nanna, will they!

MARINA. People won't, but God will.

ASTROV. Yes! Thank you. Well said.

Enter VANYA *from the house. He has had a sleep after lunch and has a somewhat rumpled appearance. He sits on a garden seat and straightens his stylish tie.*

VANYA. Yes ... (*Pause.*) Yes ...

ASTROV. Had a good sleep?

VANYA. Yes ... Very good. (*Yawns.*) Ever since the professor and his wife arrived life's been all out of joint ... I've been sleeping at the wrong time, eating fancy lunches and fancy dinners, drinking wine ... It's bad for the system, all that! There was never a spare moment before – Sonya and I used to work like beavers. Now Sonya does it all on her own, while I just sleep, eat, and drink ... It's not right!

MARINA (*shaking her head*). I don't know! The professor doesn't get up till noon, and the samovar's been on the boil all morning waiting for him. When they weren't here we had dinner at one, same as everyone else. With them here it's at seven. The professor sits up at night reading and writing, and suddenly at two o'clock in the morning there's the bell ... What do they want? Tea! Wake up the servants for him, get the samovar out ... I don't know!

ASTROV. And they're going to be here for some time yet, are they?

VANYA (*whistles*). A hundred years. The professor has decided he's going to live here.

MARINA. Now here we go again! The samovar's been on the table for two hours, and they've gone off for a walk.

VANYA. They're coming, they're coming ... Don't fret yourself.

> *Voices can be heard. From the depths of the garden, returning from their walk, come* SEREBRYAKOV, YELENA, SONYA, *and* TELEGIN.

SEREBRYAKOV. Splendid, splendid ... Wonderful views.

TELEGIN. Quite remarkable, Professor.

SONYA. Tomorrow we'll make an expedition to the local forest. Would you like that, Papa?

VANYA. Tea, then, everyone!

SEREBRYAKOV. My friends, send my tea into the study, be so kind. I have one or two things still to do this afternoon.

SONYA. You're sure to enjoy the forest ...

> YELENA, SEREBRYAKOV, *and* SONYA *go off into the house.* TELEGIN *goes to the table and sits down beside* MARINA.

VANYA. An oppressively hot day, and our great scholar goes out with an umbrella, in his overcoat, gloves, and galoshes.

ASTROV. He plainly takes good care of himself.

VANYA. But what a beauty she is! What a beauty! In all my life I've never seen a woman more lovely.

TELEGIN (*to* MARINA). Whatever I do today – ride through the open fields, stroll in the shade of the garden, look at this table here – I feel pure indescribable happiness! It's enchanting weather, the birds are singing, we're all of us living in peace and harmony together. What more could we want? (*Accepting a glass of tea.*) Thank you most kindly!

VANYA (*dreamily*). Her eyes . . . A marvellous woman!

ASTROV (*to* VANYA). So, tell us something.

VANYA (*inertly*). Tell you what?

ASTROV. Nothing new?

VANYA. Not a thing. It's all old. I'm the same as I always was, or possibly worse, because I've grown idle. I don't do anything. Just grumble away like some cantankerous old codger. Mama goes babbling on like an old jackdaw about the emancipation of women, one eye on the grave, the other scanning those clever books of hers for the dawn of a new life.

ASTROV. What about the professor?

VANYA. The professor, as always, sits writing in his study from morning until far into the night. The poor paper! He'd do better to write his autobiography. What a wonderful subject he'd make! A retired professor, a dried haddock with a doctorate . . . Gout and rheumatism and migraine, and a liver swollen with envy . . . This old dried haddock lives on his first wife's estate – much against his will – because he can't afford to live in town. He complains endlessly about his misfortune, although in actual fact he's quite unusually fortunate. (*Irritably.*) Just consider for a moment exactly how fortunate. The son of a lowly sacristan – but he went to a seminary, he took various degrees, he got a chair, he joined the upper ranks of society, he became the son-in-law of a senator, and so on and so forth. Leave all that aside, though. Just consider this. A man spends precisely twenty-five years reading and writing about Art when he understands precisely nothing about it. For twenty-five years he chews over other men's thoughts about realism and naturalism and every other kind of rubbish. For twenty-five years he reads and writes about things that clever people have known for years already, and that stupid people don't care about anyway. For twenty-five years, in other words, he's been shovelling a lot of nothing from here to nowhere. And yet what an opinion he has of himself! What pretensions! He's reached retiring age, and not a soul has ever heard of him. He's completely unknown. So for twenty-five years he's been usurping another's rightful place. Yet lo and behold – he paces the earth like a demi-god!

ASTROV. I do believe you're jealous.

VANYA. Yes, I'm jealous! And his success with women! Far greater than any Don Juan has ever known! His first wife, my sister – a lovely tender creature, as pure as the blue sky up there, with a noble heart and a generous soul, and more admirers than he's had pupils – she loved him the way only the angels can, when they love beings as fine and pure as themselves. Our mother still worships him, still walks in holy terror of him. His second wife, a beautiful, intelligent woman – you saw her just now – she married him when he was an old man already, and gave him her youth and beauty, her freedom, her radiance. Why? For what in return?

ASTROV. Is she faithful to the professor?

VANYA. Regrettably she is.

ASTROV. Why regrettably?

VANYA. Because this faithfulness of hers is false through and through. Much rhetoric in it but little logic. Deceiving an aged husband you can't bear the sight of – that's immoral; attempting to stifle your own hapless youth and living feelings – that's not immoral.

TELEGIN (*plaintively*). Vanya, I don't like it when you say that kind of thing. Really, now . . . A man who deceives his wife or a woman who betrays her husband – that's someone who can't be trusted – someone who might betray his country!

VANYA (*irritated*). Oh, do dry up, Ilyusha!

TELEGIN. Let me have my say, Vanya. My wife ran off with her fancy man the day after our wedding because of my pockmarked appearance. From that day forth I've never broken my bond. I still love her, I'm still faithful to her, I help her in so far as I'm able, I've spent all I possessed on bringing up the children she had by her fancy man. I've been deprived of happiness, but I do have my pride left. What can she say? Her youth is gone, her beauty has faded in accordance with the laws of nature, her fancy man is dead . . . What does she have left?

Enter SONYA *and* YELENA. *A moment later* MARIA VASILYEVNA *enters with a book. She sits down and reads, is served with tea and drinks it without looking.*

SONYA (*to* MARINA, *hurriedly*). Nanna, the peasants have come. Go and have a word with them – I'll do the tea . . . (*Pours tea.*)

MARINA *goes off.* YELENA *takes her cup and drinks it sitting on the swing.*

ASTROV (*to* YELENA). I'm here to see your husband, you realize. You wrote to say he was very ill, that he had rheumatism and so on. But he turns out to be perfectly well.
YELENA. Yesterday evening he was in very low spirits – he was complaining of pains in his legs. But today he's all right . . .
ASTROV. Meanwhile I've come galloping eighteen miles. Well, no matter – it's not the first time. Anyway, I'll stay the night, so at least I'll get a proper dose of sleep.
SONYA. Wonderful. It's such a rare thing for you to spend the night here. I don't suppose you've had dinner?
ASTROV. No, ma'am, I haven't.
SONYA. Then you can very conveniently have dinner here. We dine at seven these days. (*Drinks.*) Cold tea!
TELEGIN. The samovar has lost a lot of its heat by this time.
YELENA. Never mind, Ivan Ivanych. We can drink it cold just as well.
TELEGIN. Excuse me, but not Ivan Ivanych. Sorry, but it's Ilya Ilich . . . Ilya Ilich Telegin. I'm Sonya's godfather, and the Professor, your husband, knows me very well. Sorry, but I live here now, you see, on this estate . . . You may have been kind enough to notice me having dinner with you every day.
SONYA. He's our great tower of strength, our right-hand man. (*Tenderly.*) Come on, Godfather, I'll give you some more tea.

MARIA VASILYEVNA. Oh!

SONYA. What's the matter, Grandmama?

MARIA VASILYEVNA. I forgot to tell Alexandre . . . I'm quite losing my memory . . . I had a letter today from Pavel Alekseyevich in Kharkov . . . He sent his new pamphlet . . .

ASTROV. Anything interesting?

MARIA VASILYEVNA. Interesting, yes, but somehow rather curious. He's attacking the very things that he was defending seven years ago. It's quite appalling!

VANYA. Nothing's appalling. Drink your tea, *maman.*

MARIA VASILYEVNA. But I want to talk!

VANYA. But we've been talking and talking and reading pamphlets for fifty years. It's time we stopped.

MARIA VASILYEVNA. You've taken a dislike to the sound of my voice for some reason. Forgive me, Jean, but this last year you have changed out of all recognition . . . You used to be someone with clear convictions, an example of enlightenment . . .

VANYA. Oh, yes! I was an example of enlightenment that no one ever got any light from . . . (*Pause.*) An example of enlightenment . . . You couldn't have made a crueller joke! I'm forty-seven now. Until last year I was just like you – deliberately trying to blind myself with all this theory of yours, so as not to see the reality of life – and I thought I was doing the right thing. Now, though – oh, if only you knew! I can't sleep at night for spleen and anger that I've so stupidly wasted my time, when I could have had everything I now can't because of my age!

SONYA. Uncle Vanya, you're being boring!

MARIA VASILYEVNA (*to her son*). You seem to be making some kind of accusation against your former convictions . . . But it's not the convictions which are to blame – it's you. You failed to keep in mind that convictions are nothing in themselves, mere words . . . You should have got down to business.

VANYA. We can't all be perpetual writing machines, like your Herr Professor.

MARIA VASILYEVNA. What do you mean by that, pray?

SONYA (*imploringly*). Grandmama! Uncle Vanya! I implore you!

VANYA. Not another word. Wordless apologies.

Pause.

YELENA. Nice weather today, though ... Not too hot ...

Pause.

VANYA. Nice weather for hanging yourself ...

TELEGIN *strums on the guitar.* MARINA *goes by the house calling the chickens.*

MARINA. Cheep, cheep, cheep ...

SONYA. Nanna, what were the peasants here for?

MARINA. Same old thing – about that piece of waste ground. Cheep, cheep, cheep ...

SONYA. Which one are you after?

MARINA. Speckles. She's gone off with her chicks ... I don't want the crows getting them ...

Exit MARINA. TELEGIN *plays a polka; they all listen in silence. Enter a* WORKMAN.

WORKMAN. The doctor – is he here? (*to* ASTROV.) Begging your pardon, sir, but they've sent over for you.

ASTROV. Where from?

WORKMAN. The factory.

ASTROV (*with annoyance*). Oh, thank you very much indeed. I suppose I'll have to go ... (*Looks round for his cap.*) What a bore, damn it ...

SONYA. It's a shame, isn't it ... Come back for dinner afterwards.

ASTROV. No, it'll be too late by that time. (*To the* WORKMAN.) Listen, be a good chap and fetch me a glass of vodka.

Exit WORKMAN.

(*Finds his cap.*) In some play by Ostrovsky there's a man with large moustaches and small abilities. That's me. Well, goodbye to everyone ... (*To* YELENA.) If you felt like

looking in on me at any time – you could come with Sonya
here – it would give me real pleasure. I have a small estate –
eighty acres or so, but if you're interested there's a nursery
and a model orchard, the like of which you won't find for
many hundred miles around. I have the state forest next
door to me . . . The Warden there is old and ailing, so in fact
I run it all.

YELENA. Yes, people have told me you've got a great passion
for forests. Very valuable work, of course, but it must surely
interfere with your real vocation. After all, you are a doctor.

ASTROV. God alone knows what our real vocation is.

YELENA. It's interesting, though, is it?

ASTROV. Yes, it's an interesting business.

VANYA (*ironically*). Oh, highly!

YELENA (*to* ASTROV). You're still a young man – what, thirty-
six, thirty-seven, by the look of you – and it can't be as
interesting as you say. Just trees and more trees. Monoto-
nous, I should think.

SONYA. No, it's extremely interesting. The doctor plants new
woodlands every year – they've sent him a bronze medal and
a diploma for it. He makes great efforts to stop people
destroying the existing forests. Just listen to him and you'll
agree with every word. He says that forests adorn the earth,
that they teach man to appreciate beauty and give him an
intimation of majesty. Forests moderate the harshness of the
climate. And in countries with a gentle climate human beings
spend less of their strength on the struggle with nature; they
become gentler in their turn. In places like that people are
lithe and beautiful, with quick responses, and well-turned
speech, and graceful movements. Their arts and sciences
flourish, their philosophy is never sombre, they treat women
with grace and honour . . .

VANYA (*laughing*). Bravo, bravo . . . ! This is all very fine, but
it fails to convince. (*To* ASTROV.) So with your permission,
my friend, I shall continue to build my outhouses of wood
and burn wood in my stoves.

ASTROV. You can burn peat in your stoves, and build your
outhouses of stone. I've no objection, anyway, to cutting the

forests to meet our needs, but why destroy them? The Russian forests are ringing beneath the axe; thousands of millions of trees are perishing; the habitats of animals and birds are being laid waste; rivers are dwindling and drying up; marvellous landscapes are vanishing beyond recall; and all because man in his idleness hasn't sense enough to bend down and pick up his fuel from the earth. (*To* YELENA.) Isn't that the truth? Only a reckless barbarian would burn that beauty in his stove, and destroy what we cannot replace. Man is endowed with reason and creative powers to increase and multiply his inheritance, yet up to now he has created nothing, only destroyed. The forests grow ever fewer; the rivers parch; the wild life is gone; the climate is ruined; and with every passing day the earth becomes uglier and poorer. (*To* VANYA.) You sit there looking at me ironically, you don't take me seriously, and . . . and yes, perhaps it is indeed just another of my odd ideas, but when I go past trees on the peasants' land, trees that I have saved from being cut down, or when I hear the sigh and rustle of my young woodlands, planted with my own hands, then I know that I have some slight share in controlling the climate, and that if a thousand years from now human beings are happy then it will be just a tiny bit my fault. When I plant a birch tree and then see it green and swaying in the wind my heart fills with pride, and I . . .

Sees the WORKMAN, *who has brought a glass of vodka on a tray.*

However . . . (*Drinks.*) I must go. It's probably all some crackbrained notion, anyway. Goodbye!

He goes towards the house. SONYA *takes his arm and goes with him.*

SONYA. When will you come and see us again?
ASTROV. I don't know . . .
SONYA. Another month from now . . . ?

ASTROV *and* SONYA *go off into the house.* MARIA

VASILYEVNA *and* TELEGIN *remain by the table.* YELENA *and* VANYA *go towards the verandah.*

YELENA. You were being impossible again. Did you have to annoy your mother, did you have to talk about perpetual writing machines? And at lunch today you quarrelled with my husband again. So petty!

VANYA. But if I hate him?

YELENA. There's no call to hate him – he's the same as everyone else. He's no worse than you.

VANYA. If you could see the way you look, the way you move . . . The indolence of your life! The sheer indolence of it!

YELENA. The indolence, yes, and the tedium! Everyone's rude about my husband, everyone looks at me with pity – oh, the poor thing, she's got an elderly husband! All this sympathy for me – oh, I know exactly what it's about! It's the same as Astrov was saying just now: you recklessly destroy forests, all of you, and soon there won't be anything left standing on the face of the earth. You do exactly the same with human beings – you recklessly destroy them, and soon, thanks to you, there will be neither faithfulness nor innocence left in the world, nor any capacity for self-sacrifice. Why do you have to lose your head at the sight of any woman who doesn't belong to you? Because – the doctor was right – in all of you there lurks a demon of destruction. You've no pity for forests, nor for birds, nor for women, nor for one another . . .

VANYA. I don't care for all this philosophizing!

Pause.

YELENA. You could see the tension and the fatigue in that doctor's face. An interesting face. Sonya likes him, obviously – she's in love with him and I can see why. He's been here three times already since I arrived, but I'm too timid – I haven't once talked to him properly or been nice to him. He's got it into his head I'm an evil woman. The reason you and I are friends, probably, is because we're both such dull

and tedious people! Tedious, the pair of us! Don't look at me
that way – I don't like it.

VANYA. How can I look at you any other way if I'm in love
with you? You're my happiness, you're life, you're my
youth! I know the chance that you might feel the same is
negligible – nil, in fact. But there's nothing I want from you
– just let me look at you, let me listen to your voice . . .

YELENA. Sh, people might hear!

They go into the house.

VANYA (*following her*). Let me talk about my love – don't
drive me away – and that alone will be the summit of
happiness for me . . .

YELENA. It's such a torment . . .

They both go off into the house. TELEGIN *strikes the
strings and plays a polka.* MARIA VASILYEVNA *makes a
note of something in the margins of the pamphlet.*

CURTAIN

Act Two

The dining-room in SEREBRYAKOV's *house. Night. The* WATCHMAN *can be heard knocking in the garden.*

SEREBRYAKOV *sits dozing in an armchair by the open window.* YELENA *sits beside him, also dozing.*

SEREBRYAKOV (*waking*). Who is it? You, Sonya?

YELENA. Me.

SEREBRYAKOV. Oh, you ... Unbearable pain!

YELENA. Your rug's fallen on the floor. (*Tucks his legs up.*) I'll shut the window.

SEREBRYAKOV. No, I'm stifling ... I dozed off just then and dreamed I had someone else's left leg. I woke up with this agonizing pain. And no, it's not gout – it's more like rheumatism. What time is it?

YELENA. Twenty past twelve.

Pause.

SEREBRYAKOV. Look in the library tomorrow morning, will you, and see if you can find a Batyushkov. I think we've got one.

YELENA. Um?

SEREBRYAKOV. I want you to find me a complete Batyushkov in the morning. I remember we used to have one. But why is it so difficult to get my breath?

YELENA. You're tired. You didn't sleep last night, either.

SEREBRYAKOV. They say Turgenev had gout and it turned into angina. I'm afraid I might get it. Oh, this damned, disgusting business of being old! Curse it, curse it! When I got old I became offensive to myself. And all of you must find it offensive to look at me.

YELENA. You talk about being old as if it's all our fault.

SEREBRYAKOV. You're the one who finds me most offensive of all.

YELENA *moves and sits herself some way off.*

And of course you're right. I'm not a fool – I understand.
You're young, you're healthy, you're beautiful, you want to
live your life; while I'm an old man, practically a corpse. Do
you think I don't understand? And of course it's idiotic that
I'm still alive. Just wait, though – I shall release you all soon
enough. I shan't have to drag on much longer.

YELENA. I'm exhausted . . . For the love of God be quiet.

SEREBRYAKOV. Everyone's exhausted, apparently, everyone's
bored, everyone's wasting his youth, and all because of me,
while I'm the only one who's having a good time. Oh, of
course! Naturally!

YELENA. Stop it! You're tormenting me to death!

SEREBRYAKOV. I'm tormenting everyone to death. Of course.

YELENA (*on the verge of tears*). It's unbearable! Just tell me
what you want of me!

SEREBRYAKOV. Nothing.

YELENA. Then stop it. I beg you.

SEREBRYAKOV. It's curious, though, isn't it – if my brother-in-
law opens his mouth, or that old idiot of a mother of his,
that's fine, everyone listens. But if I so much as breathe a
word everyone starts to feel miserable. Even my voice is
offensive. All right, so I'm offensive, I'm an egotist, I'm a
tyrant – but don't I have some right in my old age to a little
egotism? Haven't I earned it? Don't I have a right, I ask you,
to some peace in my declining years, to some attention from
people?

YELENA. No one's disputing your rights.

The window bangs in the wind.

The wind's got up. I'm going to close the window. (*She
closes it.*) It's going to start raining any moment. No one is
disputing your rights.

Pause. In the garden the WATCHMAN *knocks and sings a
song.*

SEREBRYAKOV. You spend your life in the pursuit of learning,
you grow accustomed to the study and the lecture-hall and
distinguished colleagues – and then suddenly, without rhyme

or reason, you wake up in this crypt, seeing stupid people every day and listening to banal conversation . . . I want to live, I like success, I like being well-known and making a stir. I might as well be in Siberia. Yearning for the past all the time, following other people's successes, being frightened of dying . . . I can't do it! It's not in me! And then on top of it all to find that people won't forgive me for being old!

YELENA. Just wait, just be patient; in five or six years I shall be old as well.

Enter SONYA.

SONYA. Papa, you were the one who had Dr Astrov sent for, and now he's come you won't see him. It's very thoughtless. You've disturbed someone quite needlessly.

SEREBRYAKOV. What use is he to me, this Astrov of yours? He knows as much about medicine as I do about astronomy.

SONYA. We can't fetch the entire medical profession here for your gout.

SEREBRYAKOV. Well, I'm not going to talk to some kind of holy fool.

SONYA. Please yourself. (*Sits.*) It makes no difference to me.

SEREBRYAKOV. What time is it?

YELENA. Getting on for one.

SEREBRYAKOV. Stifling . . . Sonya, give me the drops on the table.

SONYA. Here. (*Gives him the drops.*)

SEREBRYAKOV (*irritably*). Oh, not those! No good asking anyone to do anything!

SONYA. Now, please, don't start playing up. Some people may enjoy it, but don't inflict it on me, thank you very much. I don't like it. I haven't time anyway. I've got to be up early – I've got the haymaking.

Enter VANYA, *wearing a dressing-gown and carrying a candle.*

VANYA. We're going to have a storm.

Lightning.

There! Yelena, Sonya – go to bed. I've come to take over.

SEREBRYAKOV (*alarmed*). No, no! Don't leave me with him! No! He'll just keep talking to me!

VANYA. But they must have a break! This is the second night they've been up!

SEREBRYAKOV. Let them go to bed, then, but you go away, too. Please. I implore you. We used to be friends, remember – no arguments. We'll talk another time.

VANYA (*smiling*). We used to be friends . . . Used to be . . .

SONYA. Be quiet, Uncle Vanya.

SEREBRYAKOV (*to his wife*). My dear, don't leave me with him! He'll go on and on at me.

VANYA. This is becoming slightly ludicrous.

Enter MARINA, *carrying a candle.*

SONYA. You should be in bed, Nanna. It's the middle of the night.

MARINA. Fine chance of that. The samovar's still on the table.

SEREBRYAKOV. No one getting any sleep, everyone worn to a shadow – just me having the time of my life.

MARINA (*going up to* SEREBRYAKOV, *gently*). What's the matter, then, my dear? Hurts, does it? I've got an ache in my legs myself, such an ache. (*Puts his rug straight.*) You've had this trouble a long time. The old mistress, Sonya's mother, couldn't sleep at night for grieving . . . She loved you with all her heart . . . (*Pause.*) Old people, they're like children – they want someone to feel sorry for them, but no one's sorry for you when you're old.

Kisses SEREBRYAKOV's *shoulder.*

Off we go to bed, my dear . . . Off we go, my love . . . I'll make you some lime tea – I'll warm up those feet of yours . . . I'll pray to God for you . . .

SEREBRYAKOV (*touched*). Off we go, then, Marina.

MARINA. I've got an ache in my legs, too, such an ache.

Takes him off, accompanied by SONYA.

Yes, she did nothing but grieve, the old mistress, she did nothing but weep . . . You were still little then, Sonya, you didn't understand . . . Come on, my dear, come on . . .

Exeunt SEREBRYAKOV, SONYA, *and* MARINA.

YELENA. I'm at my wits' end with him. I can scarcely stay on my feet.

VANYA. You're at your wits' end with him – I'm at my wits' end with myself. This is the third night in a row I haven't slept.

YELENA. Things have come to a fine pass in this house. Your mother hates everything and everyone except her pamphlets and the professor; the professor's on edge because he doesn't trust me and he's afraid of you; Sonya's angry with her father and angry with me – she hasn't spoken to me for the last fortnight; you hate my husband and you openly despise your own mother; *I'm* on edge – I must have burst into tears about twenty times today . . . A fine state this house is in.

VANYA. Let's leave the philosophizing!

YELENA. You're an intelligent, educated man. I should have thought you must realize that the end of the world won't be in fire and slaughter – it will be in enmity and hatred, in all these petty quarrels . . . Your task should be not recrimination but reconciliation.

VANYA. Reconcile me first with myself! My dear . . .

He presses his lips to her hand.

YELENA. Let go! (*Takes her hand away.*) Go away!

VANYA. Soon the rain will be over, and everything in nature will revive and breathe a sigh of relief. The only thing the storm won't revive is me. Day and night the same thought chokes me like a demon sitting on my chest – that my life is lost beyond recall. There's no past – that was squandered on things of no importance – and the present is horrible in its absurdity. That's my life for you, and my love; where can I put them, what can I do with them? My feelings are running to waste as pointlessly as a ray of sunshine in a bottomless pit. I'm running to waste myself.

YELENA. When you tell me about your love I feel a kind of dullness settle over me, and no words come. I'm sorry, there's nothing I can say to you. (*Makes to go.*) Good night.

VANYA (*blocking her way*). And then if only you knew how

painful it is to think that beside me in this very house
another life is running to waste – yours! What are you
waiting for? What cursed philosophy is stopping you?
Listen, just listen . . .

YELENA (*starting at him*). You're drunk!

VANYA. Possibly, possibly . . .

YELENA. Where's the doctor?

VANYA. In there . . . He's staying the night in my room.
Possibly, possibly . . . All things are possible!

YELENA. You were drinking again today? Why do you do it?

VANYA. At least it gives a semblance of life . . . Don't try to
stop me, Yelena!

YELENA. You never drank before and you never talked so
much . . . Go to bed! I'm tired of you.

VANYA (*pressing his lips to her hand*). My dear . . . you
wonderful woman!

YELENA (*with annoyance*). Leave me alone. It really is
becoming offensive.

Exit YELENA.

VANYA (*alone*). She's gone . . . (*Pause.*) Ten years ago I used to
meet her at my sister's. She was seventeen then, and I was
thirty-seven. Why didn't I fall in love with her then and
propose to her? It would have been so easy! And now she
would have been my wife . . . Yes . . . We should both have
been woken by the storm tonight; she would have been
frightened of the thunder, and I should have put my arms
round her and whispered: 'Don't be afraid, I'm here.' Oh,
wonderful thoughts! So sweet I can't help laughing . . . but
such a muddle they're making inside my head . . . Why am I
old? Why can't she understand what I'm trying to tell her?
Those rhetorical tricks of hers, the indolent moralizing, her
silly indolent thoughts about the end of the world – I find all
that deeply repellent. (*Pause.*) Oh, I've been so duped! I
worshipped that man, that miserable gout-ridden professor,
I worked like an ox for him! Sonya and I squeezed every last
drop out of his estate; we haggled over peas and curds and
sunflower oil like a couple of bargaining peasants; we went
short ourselves so as to make kopecks into rubles and send

them to him. I was proud of him and his learning – I lived and breathed him! Every word he wrote or uttered seemed to me touched with genius . . . But, oh God – now? Here he is, retired, and the sum total of his life is revealed: when he is gone not one solitary page of all his labour will remain – he's utterly unknown – he's nothing! A soap bubble! And I have been duped . . . I see that – duped like an idiot . . .

Enter ASTROV *in a frock-coat, but without waistcoat or tie, and slightly drunk. He is followed by* TELEGIN *with his guitar.*

ASTROV. Play!
TELEGIN. They're all asleep!
ASTROV. Play!

TELEGIN *strums quietly.*

(*to* VANYA). All on your own in here? No ladies? (*Puts his hands on his hips and sings quietly.*) It was the storm that woke me up. Fair drop of rain. What's the time?
VANYA. God knows.
ASTROV. I thought I heard the professor's wife.
VANYA. She was in here just now.
ASTROV. Magnificent woman. (*Examines the medicine bottles on the table.*) Medicines. Every prescription under the sun! Labels from Kharkov and Moscow and Tula . . . He's inflicted his gout on every city in the land. Is he ill or is he putting it on?
VANYA. He's ill.

Pause.

ASTROV. Why are you so miserable today? Feeling sorry for the professor, are you?
VANYA. Leave me alone.
ASTROV. Or are you in love with Mrs Professor?
VANYA. I regard her as a friend.
ASTROV. Got to that, has it?
VANYA. What do you mean, 'got to that'?
ASTROV. A woman can become a man's friend only through

the following progression: first – acquaintance; then – mistress; thereafter, certainly – friend.

VANYA. A vile piece of wisdom.

ASTROV. Is it? I suppose it is . . . I must admit, I'm becoming a rather vile sort of man. Look, I'm even drunk. I usually get drunk like this once a month. I've got the cheek of the devil when I'm in this state. I can do anything! I take on the trickiest operations and bring them off marvellously; I draw up the most far-reaching plans for the future; at times like this I don't even think there's anything odd about me – I believe I'm doing mankind some colossal service . . . Colossal! And at times like this I have my own philosophical system, and all the rest of you, my friends, are just insect-life as far as I'm concerned . . . just microbes. (*To* TELEGIN.) Play up, Ilyusha!

TELEGIN. With all my heart, old friend, but honestly – the whole house is fast asleep!

ASTROV. Play!

> TELEGIN *strums quietly.*

We could do with another drink. Come on, I think there's still some cognac left in our room. As soon as it's light we'll drive over to my place. All right?

> *Sees* SONYA *entering.*

Excuse me – I'm not wearing a tie.

> *He goes out quickly;* TELEGIN *follows him.*

SONYA. So, Uncle Vanya, you've got drunk with the doctor again. You've become drinking companions. Well, he's always been like that, but why do you have to be? It's most unfitting at your age.

VANYA. Age doesn't come into it. When there's no real life people live on illusions. It's better than nothing.

SONYA. The hay lying mown in the fields, rain every day, everything rotting – and all you can think of is illusions. You've given up the estate work entirely . . . I do it all on my own – I'm absolutely worn out . . . (*In alarm.*) Uncle, you've tears in your eyes!

VANYA. Tears? What tears? Nonsense . . . You looked at me just then like your poor dead mother. My sweet . . . (*Greedily kisses her hands and face.*) My sister . . . my sweet sister . . . Where is she now? If she had known! Oh, if she had known!

SONYA. What, Uncle? Known what?

VANYA. It's so hard to bear . . . Well, never mind . . . Later . . . Don't worry . . . I'll go away . . .

Exit VANYA.

SONYA (*knocks on the door*). Doctor! You're not asleep, are you? In here a moment!

ASTROV (*from the other side of the door*). Just coming!

A short pause, and then ASTROV *enters, now wearing waistcoat and tie.*

What is it?

SONYA. Drink yourself, if that's not something you find offensive, but don't make Uncle drink. It's bad for him.

ASTROV. Very well. We'll drink no more. (*Pause.*) I'm just going home. So that's settled. by the time they've harnessed the horses it will be dawn.

SONYA. It's raining. Wait until morning.

ASTROV. The storm's passing – I'll only catch the edge of it. I'm going. And, please, no more calls to see your father. I tell him it's gout – he tells me it's rheumatism; I tell him to stay in bed – he sits in a chair. And today he wouldn't so much as speak to me.

SONYA. He's been spoilt. (*Hunts in the sideboard.*) Would you like a bit of something?

ASTROV. Yes. Thank you.

SONYA. I love little midnight feasts. I think there's something in the sideboard. They say he had great success with women all his life, and it was the ladies who spoilt him. Here, take the cheese.

They both stand at the sideboard and eat.

ASTROV. I didn't eat today, just drank. He's a difficult man, your father. (*Gets a bottle out of the sideboard.*) May I? (*Pours a glass.*) There's no one around, so I can speak my mind. You know, I don't think I should last a month in your house – I'd suffocate in this atmosphere ... Your father, entirely taken up with his gout and his books; Uncle Vanya and his gloom; your grandmother; and then there's your stepmother ...

SONYA. What's the matter with my stepmother?

ASTROV. Everything about a person should be beautiful: their face and clothes – and their heart and mind. Would the mirror on her wall say she was fairest of them all? She just eats and sleeps and goes for little walks, and captivates us all with her looks – that's all she does. She's no responsibilities, other people do all the work for her ... Isn't that right? And a life of idleness can't be an innocent one. (*Pause.*) Well, perhaps I'm being too severe. I'm dissatisfied with life, like your Uncle Vanya, and we're turning into a pair of old grousers.

SONYA. You're not contented with life, then?

ASTROV. Life in general I love, but our life, our narrow Russian provincial life, I cannot endure – I despise it from the bottom of my soul. And as far as my own personal life goes, then God knows there's certainly nothing good about *that*. Look, if you're going through the forest on a dark night and there's a gleam of light in the distance then you don't notice how tired you are or how dark it is or how the briars keep hitting you in the face ... I work – you know this – harder than anyone in the district, it's never been easy for me. I find life intolerably painful at times; but I've no gleam of light in the distance. I don't hope for anything for myself, I don't have much love for others ... For a long time now there's been no one I've loved.

SONYA. No one?

ASTROV. No one at all. The only person I feel a certain tenderness towards is your Nanna, for old times' sake. The peasants are all alike – backward, living in filth – and there's not much common ground between them and the educated classes. Who are themselves a weariness to the soul. All of them, all our good kind friends, have petty thoughts and petty feelings. They can't see further than the end of their nose – they're just plain stupid. And those of them who are a little more intelligent, a little less paltry, are hysterical instead, and preoccupied with analysis and introspection . . . They whine, they pursue little vendettas and sick-minded slanders. They come sidling up to you and look at you out of the corner of their eye and decide: 'Oh, he's raving mad!' Or: 'Bit high-falutin, this one.' And when they don't know quite what label to stick on me they say: 'He's a strange one, he's a strange fellow!' I love the forest – that's strange: I don't eat meat – that's another strange thing. A direct, innocent, open approach to nature or people is a thing of the past . . . It doesn't exist! (*Goes to take another drink.*)

SONYA (*stops him*). No, I beg you, I implore you – don't drink any more.

ASTROV. Why not?

SONYA. It's so unworthy of you! You're a man of refinement, you're so gently-spoken . . . And not just that – you're handsome in a way that no one else I know is. So why do you want to be like ordinary people who drink and play cards? Don't do it, I implore you! You always say that people don't create, they just destroy what heaven has given them. So why, why are you destroying yourself? You mustn't, you mustn't, I implore you, I entreat you.

ASTROV (*holds out his hand to her*). I'll drink no more.

SONYA. Give me your word.

ASTROV. My word of honour.

SONYA (*presses his hand tightly*). Thank you!

ASTROV. *Basta!* I've sobered up. Look, I'm completely sober, and will so remain for as long as I live. (*Looks at his watch.*) Let's go on with our conversation, then. What I'm saying is this: I've had my day, my time is past . . . I've grown old, I've worked myself too hard, I've got coarsened, my feelings are all blunted, and I don't think now I could attach myself to another human being. There's no one I love . . . and no one now I ever shall love. The thing that does still have a hold on me is beauty. I can't be indifferent to it. Your stepmother, for instance. I think if she wanted to she could turn my head in a day . . . But then that's nothing to do with love, nothing to do with attachment . . . (*Puts his hand over his eyes and shudders.*)

SONYA. What's the matter?

ASTROV. Oh . . . In Lent one of my patients died under the chloroform.

SONYA. It's time you put that out of your mind. (*Pause.*) Tell me something . . . If I had a friend, or a younger sister, and if you found out that she was . . . well, in love with you, say, how would you respond to that?

ASTROV (*shrugs*). I don't know. Not at all, I suppose. I'd make it clear to her that I couldn't love her . . . and that I'd got other things to think about. Anyway, I must go if I'm going. Goodbye, then, my dear, or we'll be here all night.

Shakes her hand.

I'll go through the drawing-room if I may – I'm afraid I may get held up by your uncle otherwise.

Exit ASTROV.

SONYA (*alone*). He didn't say anything . . . His heart and mind are still hidden from me, so why do I feel so happy? (*Laughs with happiness.*) 'You're refined,' I told him, 'you're noble, you're gently-spoken . . . ' It wasn't the wrong thing to say, was it? His voice is so vibrant and caressing – I can hear it lingering in the air. But when I said that about my younger sister he didn't understand . . . (*Wringing her hands.*) Oh, what a terrible thing it is that I'm not beautiful! What a terrible thing! Because I know I'm not beautiful – I know, I know . . . Last Sunday, as everyone was coming out of church, I heard people talking about me, and one woman said: 'She's good-hearted and kind, but it's a pity she's so plain . . . ' Plain . . .

Enter YELENA.

YELENA (*opens the windows*). The storm's over. What wonderful air! (*Pause.*) Where's the doctor?
SONYA. Gone.

   Pause.

YELENA. Sonya!
SONYA. What?
YELENA. How long are you going to go on pouting at me? We
   haven't done each other any harm. Why should we be
   enemies? Enough, now . . .
SONYA. I've been wanting to say it, too . . .

   Embraces YELENA.

No more crossness.
YELENA. That's better.

   They are both moved.

SONYA. Has Papa gone to bed?
YELENA. No, he's sitting in the drawing-room . . . We don't
   speak to each other for weeks at a time – heaven knows why
   . . . (*Sees the sideboard open.*) What's this?
SONYA. The doctor was having a bite of supper.
YELENA. There's some wine . . . Let's drink to being friends.
SONYA. Yes, why not?
YELENA. Out of the same glass . . . (*Pours.*) That will be nicer.
   So – friends?
SONYA. Friends.

   They drink and kiss each other.

I've been wanting to make up for a long time, but I kept
feeling somehow ashamed of it . . . (*Weeps.*)
YELENA. Why are you crying?
SONYA. It's nothing. Just crying.
YELENA. There now, there now . . . (*Weeps.*) You funny girl –
   now I've started to cry as well . . . (*Pause.*) You're cross with
   me because you thought I married your father for his money
   . . . If oaths mean anything to you then I'll give you my oath

I married him for love. I was fascinated by him because he was a learned and famous man. It wasn't real love, it was artificial, but I certainly thought it was real then. I'm not to blame. But from the very day of our wedding you've never ceased to punish me with those clever suspicious eyes of yours.

SONYA. Anyway, pax, pax! Let bygones be bygones, yes?

YELENA. You mustn't look at people like that, you know – it's not your style. You must trust everyone – life's impossible if you don't.

Pause.

SONYA. Tell me truly, now we're friends . . . Are you happy?

YELENA. No.

SONYA. I knew you weren't. One more question. Be frank – would you like to have a husband who was young?

YELENA. What a child you are still. Of course I should. (*Laughs.*) Go on, then, ask me something else. Go on . . .

SONYA. Do you like the doctor?

YELENA. Yes, very much.

SONYA (*laughs*). I've got a silly face on, haven't I . . . He's gone, and here I am still hearing his voice, hearing his step, looking at the dark glass in the window and thinking I can see his face there. Let me finish . . . I can't say it out loud, though – I can feel my cheeks burning. Let's go to my room – we can talk there. Do you think I'm silly? Admit it, now . . . Say something to me about him.

YELENA. Say what?

SONYA. He's a clever man . . . He can do anything . . . He's a doctor, he plants trees . . .

YELENA. It's not just a question of trees and medicine . . . Listen, my love, he's someone with real talent. You know what that means, having talent? It means being a free spirit, it means having boldness and wide horizons . . . He plants a sapling, and he has some notion what will become of it in a thousand years' time; he already has some glimpse of the millennium. Such people are rare; they must be loved . . . He drinks, he can be a little coarse at times – but what of it? A man of talent in Russia can't be a simple innocent. Just think what this doctor's life is like! Impassable mud on the roads, freezing weather, snowstorms, huge distances, crude and uncivilized peasants, disease and poverty on every hand; and in conditions like those it's hard for anyone working and struggling day after day to preserve himself to the age of forty in simple innocence and sobriety . . .

Kisses SONYA.

I wish you happiness with all my heart; you deserve it . . . (*Gets up.*) I'm a tedious person, though, a minor character . . . In music, in my husband's house, in all my romances – everywhere, in fact, that's all I've been – a minor character. In all conscience, Sonya, if you think about it, I'm very, very unhappy! (*Walks up and down in agitation.*) There's no happiness for me in this world! None! Why are you laughing?

SONYA (*laughs, covering her face*). I'm so happy . . . so happy!

YELENA. I feel like playing the piano . . . I wouldn't mind playing something now.

SONYA. Yes, do.

Embraces YELENA.

I can't sleep . . . Do play!

YELENA. In a moment. Your father isn't asleep. Music irritates him when he's ill. Go and ask him. If he doesn't mind, then yes, I'll play. Go on.

SONYA. I'm going!

Exit SONYA. *The sound of the* WATCHMAN *and his dogs in the garden.*

YELENA. I haven't played for a long time. I'll play, and I'll cry and cry like a child. (*Out of the window.*) Is that you Yefim?

WATCHMAN (*off*). Ma'am!

YELENA. Keep the dogs quiet, the master's not well.

WATCHMAN (*off*). I'll take myself off, then! (*Whistles to his dogs.*) Hey, boy! Here, boy!

Pause. SONYA *returns.*

SONYA. No!

CURTAIN

Act Three

The drawing-room in SEREBRYAKOV's house. Three doors, left, right, and centre. Day.

VANYA and SONYA, sitting. YELENA, walking round the room thinking about something.

VANYA. Herr Professor is graciously pleased to desire us all to assemble here in the drawing-room today at one o'clock. (Looks at his watch.) Quarter to one. He has something to announce to the world.

YELENA. Oh, some bit of business, I expect.

VANYA. He hasn't got any business. Writing rubbish, complaining, and being jealous – that's all the business he's got.

SONYA (reproachfully). Uncle!

VANYA. I'm sorry, I'm sorry. (Indicates YELENA.) Look at her! Reeling as she walks from sheer indolence. How charming! How very charming!

YELENA. Droning, droning on the whole day long! I wonder you don't get sick of it. (Leadenly.) I'm bored to death. I can't think what I can do.

SONYA (shrugs). There are plenty of things. If only you wanted to.

YELENA. For instance?

SONYA. Do some of the estate work – teach – treat the sick. Isn't that plenty enough? When you and Papa weren't here Uncle Vanya and I used to go to market and sell the flour.

YELENA. I don't know how to. It wouldn't be interesting, anyway. It's only in uplifting novels that people go out and teach and doctor the peasants. How can I just suddenly turn round and start teaching and doctoring?

SONYA. What I don't understand is how anyone could fail to. Give it a little while and you'll get used to it. (Embraces her.) Don't be bored, my dear. (Laughs.) You're bored – you can't find a job to do – and boredom and idleness are catching. Look: Uncle Vanya does nothing but follow you round like a shadow – and I've dropped what I was doing to come running here to talk to you. I've grown idle, and I can't afford to be! The doctor used to come and visit us only very occasionally – once a month – it was hard to persuade him; and now he comes every day – he's quite given up his trees and his practice. You must have bewitched us.

VANYA (*to* YELENA). Why are you languishing? (*Briskly.*) Use your intelligence, my dear! You have mermaid's blood in your veins – so be a mermaid! Run wild for once in your life – rush off and fall madly in love with some fellow-sprite – then splash you go, head first into a hole at the bottom of the river – while Herr Professor and all the rest of us stand helplessly looking on.

YELENA (*angrily*). Leave me alone, will you! It's so unkind!

She tries to go. He prevents her.

VANYA. Come on, now, my sweet, forgive me . . . I apologize.

Kisses her hand.

Pax.

YELENA. It would test the patience of a saint, you must admit.

VANYA. As a peace token I'll bring you a bouquet of roses – I picked them for you this morning . . . Autumn roses – lovely, mournful roses . . .

Exit VANYA.

SONYA. Autumn roses – lovely, mournful roses . . .

They both look out of the window.

YELENA. September already. We shall have to get through the winter here somehow! (*Pause.*) Where's the doctor?

SONYA. In Uncle Vanya's room. He's painting something. I'm glad Uncle Vanya's gone – I must have a word with you.

YELENA. What about?

SONYA. What about?

She lays her head on YELENA's *breast.*

YELENA. There, now, there.

She strokes SONYA's *hair.*

There, now.

SONYA. I'm not beautiful.

YELENA. You have beautiful hair.

SONYA. Don't say that! (*Looks round to glance at herself in the mirror.*) When a woman isn't beautiful people say to her: 'You have beautiful eyes, you have beautiful hair . . .' I've loved him for six years now – loved him more than my own mother. I hear his voice all the time, I feel the pressure of his hand on mine; and I look at the door and wait – I keep thinking he's going to come in any moment. And I keep running to you like this to talk about him. He comes every day now, but he doesn't look at me, he doesn't see me . . . It's such torture! I've no hope – none, none at all! (*In despair.*) I've no strength left . . . I prayed all night . . . Often I go up to him and start the conversation myself. I look him straight in the face . . . I haven't the pride, I haven't the strength to control myself . . . Yesterday I couldn't stop myself confessing to Uncle Vanya . . . And all the servants know I'm in love with him. Everyone knows.

YELENA. What about him?

SONYA. No. He never notices me.

YELENA (*thoughtfully*). He's a funny man . . . I've an idea. Let me have a talk to him . . . I'll be very discreet and I won't say anything directly . . . (*Pause.*) It's quite true – to be kept in suspense all this time . . . Let me try!

SONYA *nods.*

All right, then. Either he loves you or he doesn't – it's easy enough to find out. Now, don't worry, my pet – I'll do it very discreetly – he'll never even notice. We just want to know which it is: yes or no. (*Pause.*) If it's no, then he should stop coming here. Right?

SONYA *nods.*

It's easier when you don't see people. We won't delay, then – we'll cross-examine him forthwith. He was going to show me something he's drawing . . . Go and tell him I want to see him.

SONYA (*in great agitation*). You will tell me the whole truth?

YELENA. Of course. Whatever the truth, I think, at any rate it can't be as terrible as being in suspense. You can rely on me, my sweet.

SONYA. All right, all right . . . I'll say you want to see his drawings . . .

Starts to go, and then stops at the door.

No, better to stay in suspense . . . At least there's still hope . . .

YELENA. What's this, now?

SONYA. Nothing.

Exit SONYA.

YELENA (*alone*). Is there anything worse than knowing the secrets of another's heart and not being able to help? (*Reflects.*) He's not in love with her, that's plain enough, but why shouldn't he marry her? She's not beautiful, but for a country doctor, at his age, she'd make a fine wife. She's intelligent, she's kind and good . . . That's all beside the point, though, that's all beside the point . . . (*Pause.*) I know how it is for that poor child. In the midst of all this desperate boredom, where all the people around her are just perambulating grey blobs, where every word spoken is vile, where there's nothing going on but eating, drinking, and sleeping, *he* makes one of his occasional appearances; and he's not like the others – he's handsome, he's interesting, he's fascinating – and it's like the bright moon rising in the midst of darkness . . . To fall under the spell of a man like that, to forget oneself . . . I think I've become slightly fascinated, too. When he's not here, yes, I'm bored – and now here I am smiling at the thought of him . . . Uncle Vanya tells me I have mermaid's blood in my veins. 'Run wild for once in your life . . .' So – perhaps that's what I should do . . . Fly off as free as a bird away from all of you, away from your half-asleep faces, away from all this talk – forget your very existence . . . But I'm a coward, I'm too timid . . . I should be tormented by conscience . . . I feel guilty as it is, with his coming here every day – because I can guess why he comes – I'm already almost down on my knees in front of Sonya, weeping and begging her to forgive me . . .

Enter ASTROV *with a map.*

ASTROV. Good afternoon.

He shakes hands with her.

You wanted to see what I've been painting?

YELENA. You promised yesterday you'd show me your work . . . Can you spare the time?

ASTROV. Of course.

He spreads the map out on the card-table and fixes it with drawing-pins.

Where were you born?

YELENA (*helps him*). St Petersburg.

ASTROV. And where did you study?

YELENA. At the Conservatoire.

ASTROV. You may not find this very interesting.

YELENA. Why not? I don't know the country, it's true, but I've read a lot.

ASTROV. I've got my own work-table in the house here. In Vanya's room. When I get completely exhausted, and I can't think properly any more, I drop everything and come running over here to distract myself with this thing for an hour or two . . . Vanya and Sonya click away on the abacus, and I sit beside them at my table, busy with my colouring, and it's warm and peaceful, and the cricket chirps. I don't allow myself this pleasure very often, though – once a month . . . (*Indicates the map.*) Now, look at this. It represents this part of the country as it was fifty years ago. The light and dark green colouring indicates forest; half of the entire surface area is forest. Where the green is hatched with red there were elk and wild goats . . . I've indicated the fauna as well as the flora. On this lake there were swans and geese and ducks, and what the old people call a power of birds of every sort – the place was swarming with them. Apart from villages, look, you can see a scattering of various settlements and smallholdings, little monasteries, watermills . . . Cattle and horses were abundant. They're marked in blue. This district, for example, was thick with blue; there were complete herds, and two or three horses per farm. (*Pause.*) Now let's look down here. As it was twenty-five years ago. By this time only a third of the surface-area is under forest. The goats have gone, but there are still elk. The green and blue are paler now. And so on, and so on. Let us move on to the third section – the district as it is today. There's green here and there, but it's not solid, it's only in patches; the elk, the swans, and the capercailzies have all vanished . . . Of the former settlements, smallholdings, monasteries, and mills – not a trace. Overall it's the picture of a gradual but incontrovertible decline, which by the look of it will be complete in another ten or fifteen years. You'll tell me that civilizing factors are at work here, that the old life must naturally give way to the new. And, yes, I see that if these ruined forests had been replaced by roads and railways, if there were factories and schools here, then the peasants would be healthier and wealthier and wiser – but nothing of the kind! The district still has the same swamps and mosquitoes, the same lack of roads, the same poverty and typhus and diphtheria and fires . . . What we are faced with here is a decline resulting from the unequal struggle for existence, a decline brought about by stagnation, by ignorance, by a total lack of awareness, by frozen, sick, and hungry men who, to preserve the last flickers of life, to save their children, instinctively, blindly, grasp at anything they can use to relieve their hunger and warm themselves, and who destroy it all without thought for the morrow . . . Almost everything has been destroyed now; and nothing yet has been created in its place. (*Coldly.*) I see from your expression that you're not interested.

YELENA. I understand so little about it.

ASTROV. There's nothing to understand – you're simply not interested.

YELENA. I was thinking about something else, to tell you the truth. Forgive me. I have to subject you to a little cross-examination, and I feel somewhat awkward about it – I don't know how to begin.

ASTROV. A cross-examination?

YELENA. Yes, but . . . a rather innocent one. Let's sit down, shall we?

They sit.

YELENA. It's to do with a certain young lady. We'll be quite straightforward about this, shall we – a friendly conversation, no talking in riddles. All right?

ASTROV. All right.

YELENA. It's to do with my stepdaughter, Sonya. Do you like her?

ASTROV. Yes, I have a high regard for her.

YELENA. Do you like her as a woman?

ASTROV (*after a moment*). No.

YELENA. Just a few words more and we'll be finished. You haven't noticed anything?

ASTROV. Noticed anything?

YELENA (*takes his hand*). You don't love her, I can see it in your eyes . . . It's very painful for her. You must understand that – and stop coming here.

ASTROV (*rises*). I've had my day . . . Anyway, I've no time for all this . . . (*Shrugs.*) I haven't the time. (*He is embarrassed.*)

YELENA. Oh dear, what a disagreeable conversation! I'm so flustered – I feel as if I'd been dragging a ten-ton weight around. Anyway, we've finished, thank heavens. We'll forget this ever took place and . . . and you must leave. You're an intelligent man, you'll understand . . . (*Pause.*) I've gone quite red.

ASTROV. If you had told me this a month or two ago I might have given it some thought, but now . . . (*Shrugs.*) Still, if she finds it painful, then naturally . . . There's only one thing I don't understand, and that is why you needed this cross-examination.

He looks her in the eye and wags his finger.

You're a sly one!

YELENA. What do you mean?

ASTROV. You're being sly! All right, so Sonya finds the situation painful. I accept that – but what's the point of this cross-examination? (*Briskly, preventing her from speaking.*) Come on, now, don't put on your surprised face – you know perfectly well why I come here every day ... Why I come, and who I come to see – you know that perfectly well. My sweet sparrowhawk, I've been swooped upon before!

YELENA. Sparrowhawk? I don't understand.

ASTROV. A beautiful, silky-smooth ferret, then ... You must have victims! For a whole month now I've done nothing – I've let it all go and come thirsting after you – and you find that terribly pleasing ... So there we are. I'm sure you knew that even without any cross-examination. (*Folds his arms and bends his head.*) I submit. Take, eat!

YELENA. You've gone mad!

ASTROV (*laughs through his teeth*). You've gone bashful ...

YELENA. I'm not the sort of person you think! I swear I'm not!

She tries to go. He bars her way.

ASTROV. I'm leaving today, and I shan't come here any more, but ...

He takes her hand and looks round.

... Where are we going to meet? Tell me quickly – where? Someone may come in – quick now ... (*Passionately.*) You wonderful, magnificent woman ... One kiss ... Let me just kiss your sweet-scented hair ...

YELENA. I swear to you ...

ASTROV (*prevents her from speaking*). Why do you need to swear to me? Oh, so beautiful! Such hands!

Kisses her hands.

YELENA. Now that's enough ... Go away. (*Pulls her hands back.*) You've forgotten yourself.

ASTROV. Tell me, though, tell me – where shall we meet tomorrow?

Takes her by the waist.

You can see, it's inevitable, we must go on meeting.

Kisses her; and as he does so VANYA *enters with a bouquet of roses, and stops in the doorway.*

YELENA (*not seeing* VANYA). Have pity on me ... Leave me be ...

Lays her head on ASTROV's *chest.*

No!

She tries to go. ASTROV *restrains her by the waist.*

ASTROV. Come to the forestry office tomorrow ... about two ... All right? All right? Will you?

YELENA (*sees* VANYA). Let me go! (*Moves away towards the window in great confusion.*) This is appalling.

VANYA (*puts the bouquet down on a chair, and in his agitation mops his face and under his collar with his handkerchief*). It's all right ... Never mind ... It's all right ...

ASTROV (*with ill-grace*). Very passable weather today, my dear sir. Overcast this morning – looked like rain – sun's out now, though. We're having a beautiful autumn, it must in all honesty be said ... And the winter crops are coming along. (*Rolls the map into a tube.*) The only thing is, the days are drawing in ...

Exit ASTROV. YELENA *goes quickly across to* VANYA.

YELENA. You'll do your best, you'll use all the influence you have, to see that my husband and I get away from here today. You understand? Today!

VANYA (*wipes his face*). What? Oh, yes ... Right ... I saw it all, Yelena, I saw the whole thing ...

YELENA (*tensely*). You understand? I must be away from here
today!

Enter SEREBRYAKOV, SONYA, TELEGIN, *and* MARINA.

TELEGIN. I'm a little off-colour myself, Professor. Haven't
been right for the last couple of days. Something a bit, you
know, in my head . . .

SEREBRYAKOV. Where are the others, though? I hate this
house. It's like a maze. Twenty-six enormous rooms –
everyone goes wandering off – you can never find anyone.
(*Rings.*) Ask Maria Vasilyevna and my wife to come in, will
you.

YELENA. I'm here.

SEREBRYAKOV. Be seated, if you please, ladies and gentlemen.

SONYA *goes across to* YELENA.

SONYA (*impatiently*). What did he say?

YELENA. I'll tell you afterwards.

SONYA. You're trembling? You're upset?

Searches YELENA's *face.*

I see . . . He said he wouldn't come here any more . . . Am I
right? (*Pause.*) Tell me – am I right?

YELENA *nods.*

SEREBRYAKOV (*to* TELEGIN). A man can put up with ill-
health, hard as that may be. What I cannot bear is the whole
tenor of rural life. I feel as if I'd fallen off the earth on to
some alien planet. Be seated, ladies and gentlemen, I beg of
you. Sonya! (*Pause.*) She's deaf. (*To* MARINA.) You, too,
Nanna – sit down.

MARINA *sits down and knits a stocking.*

Ladies and gentlemen. Lend me your ears, if I may so
express myself, and they shall be with interest returned unto
you. (*Laughs.*)

VANYA (*agitatedly*). You don't need me, perhaps? May I go?

SEREBRYAKOV. On the contrary, I need you most of all.

VANYA. Why? What for?

SEREBRYAKOV. A little unfriendly, your manner . . . Why are you angry? (*Pause.*) If I have in some way offended against you, please – forgive me.

VANYA. Oh, not that tone of voice! Let's get down to it. What do you want?

Enter MARIA VASILYEVNA.

SEREBRYAKOV. And here is *maman*. I will begin, then. (*Pause.*) I have asked you to come here today, ladies and gentlemen, to tell you that the Inspector-General is on his way. Joking aside, however. The matter is a serious one. I have assembled you all, ladies and gentlemen, to seek your help and counsel. And knowing as I do your unfailing kindness, I believe I shall not be disappointed. The world I inhabit is the world of learning, the world of books, and I have ever been a stranger to the practical life. I cannot manage without the guidance of people who know their way around in these matters, and I am looking to you, Vanya, and (*to* TELEGIN) to you, my friend, and to you, *maman* . . . The point is that *manet omnes una nox*, the same night awaits us all, which is to say that we are all in the hands of God. I am old and ailing, and I therefore think it fit to set my affairs in order insofar as they affect my family. My own life is over – it is not myself I am thinking of; but I have a young wife and an unmarried daughter. (*Pause.*) It is impossible for me to go on living in the country. We were not created for the country. It is equally impossible, though, to live in town on the kind of revenues that we receive from this estate. If we were to sell our forest, let us say, that would be an extraordinary measure which we could not adopt every year. Ways must be sought of guaranteeing us a permanent and more or less fixed amount of income. I have thought of one such way, and beg leave to present it for your consideration. I shall set it forth in outline; the details later. Our estate yields an average return of no more than two per cent. I propose to sell it. If we invest the money which this produces in stocks and shares then we shall earn between four and five

per cent, and there will, I believe, be even a surplus of some
few thousand rubles which will enable us to purchase a
modest villa within reasonable distance of St Petersburg.

VANYA. Wait a moment . . . I think my hearing must be going.
Repeat what you just said.

SEREBRYAKOV. Invest the money in stocks and shares and use
the surplus that remains to buy a villa near St Petersburg.

VANYA. Not about St Petersburg . . . You said something else.

SEREBRYAKOV. I propose to sell the estate.

VANYA. That was it. You're going to sell the estate – wonderful
– brilliant idea . . . But what do you want *us* to do with
ourselves – me and my aged mother and Sonya here?

SEREBRYAKOV. All this we shall go into at the proper time.
Not now.

VANYA. Wait a moment. I've evidently been walking round up
to now in a state of complete idiocy. Up to now I was stupid
enough to believe that this estate belonged to Sonya. My late
father purchased it as a dowry for my sister. Up to now I
supposed in my naivety that we were not living under
Turkish law, and that from my sister the estate had passed to
Sonya.

SEREBRYAKOV. Yes, the estate belongs to Sonya. No one is
disputing that. Without Sonya's consent I shall take no
decision about selling it. I am, in any case, proposing to do
this for Sonya's benefit.

VANYA. This is past all comprehending! Either I've gone mad,
or . . . or . . .

MARIA VASILYEVNA. Jean, *il ne faut pas le contredire*. Believe
me, Alexandre knows what's right and what's wrong better
than we do.

VANYA. No, give me some water. (*Drinks water.*) Go ahead –
say anything you like!

SEREBRYAKOV. I don't understand why you're getting excited.
I'm not saying my plan is ideal. If everyone finds it
inappropriate I shan't insist.

Pause.

TELEGIN (*in embarrassment*). I have a profound reverence for learning, Professor, but I have something more – I have family feeling. My brother's wife's brother, you may perhaps know him, held a master's degree . . .

VANYA. Wait a moment, Ilyusha, we've got business to deal with. Later, afterwards . . . (*To* SEREBRYAKOV.) Ask *him*. The estate was purchased from his uncle.

SEREBRYAKOV. What would be the point of my asking? What would it tell us?

VANYA. This estate was purchased at the going rate then for ninety-five thousand rubles. My father paid only seventy thousand down, and the other twenty-five were carried as a debt. Now, listen to me . . . This estate would never have been bought at all if I had not renounced my inheritance in favour of my sister, whom I loved most passionately. On top of which I worked like an ox for ten years and paid off the entire debt . . .

SEREBRYAKOV. I'm sorry I ever started this conversation.

VANYA. The estate is clear of debt and in working order thanks purely to my own personal efforts. And now I've got old I'm to be thrown out on my neck!

SEREBRYAKOV. I don't understand what you're driving at!

VANYA. For twenty-five years I have run this estate, I have worked, and I have sent you the money, like the most conscientious of bailiffs, and not once in all that time have you offered me a word of thanks. From start to finish – from when I was young until the present day – you have paid me the princely salary of five hundred rubles a year – and not once has it entered your head to give me a single ruble more!

SEREBRYAKOV. How was I to know? I'm not a practical man – I don't understand these things. You could have given yourself more – as much as you liked.

VANYA. Why didn't I steal? Why don't you all despise me for not stealing? It would have been no more than simple justice, and I shouldn't be a beggar now!

MARIA VASILYEVNA (*sternly*). Jean!

TELEGIN. Don't Vanya, don't! My dear old friend . . . ! I'm shaking . . . Why spoil good relations?

Kisses him.

Don't do it.

VANYA. For twenty-five years I have been shut up between four walls with this mother of mine like a mole in the dark ... All our thoughts and feelings were centred on you. The days we spent talking about you and your works, being proud of you, uttering your name in reverential tones; the nights we blighted reading books and journals for which I now feel nothing but profound contempt!

TELEGIN. Don't, Vanya, don't ... I can't bear it ...

SEREBRYAKOV (*with rage*). I don't understand what it is you want.

VANYA. We thought you were some kind of superior being – we knew your articles by heart ... But now my eyes have been opened! I see it all! You write about art, but you've not the slightest understanding of art! All those works of yours that I used to love – they're not worth a brass button! You've made fools of us!

SEREBRYAKOV. Everyone – please! Make him see reason! I'm going!

YELENA (*to* VANYA). I insist you be silent! Do you hear?

VANYA. I won't be silent!

Bars SEREBRYAKOV's *way.*

Wait, I haven't finished! You've blighted my life! I haven't lived, I haven't lived! Through your kind efforts I have destroyed the best years of my life! You're my worst enemy!

TELEGIN. I can't bear this ... I can't ... I'm going ...

Exit TELEGIN *in great agitation.*

SEREBRYAKOV. What do you want of me? And what right do you have to take that tone with me? A little nobody like you! If the estate belongs to you then take it – I don't need it!

YELENA. I'm not staying another moment in this hell! (*Shouts.*) I can't endure it any longer!

VANYA. My life has vanished! I have the talent, I have the brains, I have the nerve ... If I had led a normal life I could have been a Schopenhauer, I could have been a Dostoyevsky

... I don't know what I'm saying! I'm going mad ...
Mother, I'm in despair! Mother!

MARIA VASILYEVNA (*sternly*). Do as Alexandre tells you!

SONYA *kneels in front of* MARINA *and clings to her.*

SONYA. Nanna! Nanna!

VANYA. Mother! What am I going to do? No, don't say
anything, there's no need! I know what I'm going to do! (*To*
SEREBRYAKOV.) I'll give you something to remember me by!

Exit VANYA *through the centre door.* MARIA VASI-
LYEVNA *goes after him.*

SEREBRYAKOV. In heaven's name, what is all this? Get this
madman away from me! I can't stay under the same roof!
He lives in there ... (*Indicates the centre door.*) ... almost
on top of me ... Let him move into the village, or into the
lodge, or *I'll* move out, but remain in the same house as him
I cannot ...

YELENA (*to her husband.*) We're leaving today! You must give
orders at once.

SEREBRYAKOV. An absolute little nobody!

SONYA, *on her knees, turns to her father.*

SONYA (*agitatedly, on the verge of tears*). You must be
merciful, Papa! Uncle Vanya and I are so unhappy!
(*Restraining her despair.*) You must be merciful! Remember
when you were younger how Uncle Vanya and Grandmother
used to work at night translating books for you, copying
your papers ... Whole nights they spent, whole nights
together! Uncle Vanya and I have worked without rest – we
were afraid to spend a kopeck on ourselves – we sent
everything to you ... We stinted our bread! I'm not saying
the right things, it's coming out all wrong, but you should
understand our feelings, Papa. You must be merciful!

YELENA (*to her husband, disturbed*). For the love of God,
make it up with him ... I implore you.

SEREBRYAKOV. Very well, I'll make it up with him ... I'm not
blaming him, I'm not angry, but you must agree that his

behaviour is a little odd, to say the least. If you'll excuse me, then, I'll go and have a word with him.

Exit SEREBRYAKOV *through the centre door.*

YELENA. Be a little gentler with him – soothe him down . . .

Exit YELENA *after him.*

SONYA (*clinging to* MARINA). Nanna! Nanna!

MARINA. Never you mind, now, child. The geese will have their cackle, then they'll quieten . . . Cackle and quieten, cackle and quieten . . .

SONYA. Nanna!

MARINA (*strokes her hair*). You're shivering as though you'd been out in the freezing cold! There, now, you poor orphan child, God will have mercy. A drop of lime tea, or raspberry, now, and you'll feel better . . . Don't grieve, child . . . (*Looking at the centre door, feelingly.*) You see? They've quietened down, those old geese, drat them!

A shot, off. YELENA *is heard to scream.* SONYA *shudders.*

Oh, heaven preserve us!

SEREBRYAKOV *runs in, reeling in alarm.*

SEREBRYAKOV. Stop him! Restrain him! He's gone mad!

YELENA *and* VANYA *struggle in the doorway.*

YELENA (*trying to take the revolver away from him*). Give it me! Give it me, I tell you!

VANYA. Let go! Let go of me!

He breaks free, runs into the room, and looks around for SEREBRYAKOV.

Where is he? Ah, there he is!

Fires at him.

Bang! (*Pause.*) Didn't I hit him? Another botch-up? (*With rage.*) Oh, hell, hell . . . hell and damnation . . .

Hammers on the floor with the revolver, and sinks exhausted into a chair. SEREBRYAKOV *is stunned.* YELENA *leans against the wall, about to faint.*

YELENA. Take me away from this place! Take me away, kill me, anything, but . . . I can't stay in this place – I can't!

VANYA (*in despair*). Oh, what am I doing? What am I doing?

SONYA (*quietly*). Nanna! Nanna!

CURTAIN

Act Four

VANYA's *room. It serves both as his bedroom and as the estate office. By the window is a large table with account books and papers of various sorts; a high counting-house desk; cupboards and scales. There is a somewhat smaller table for* ASTROV *with paints and drawing materials on it, and a portfolio beside it. A starling in a cage. On the wall hangs a map of Africa, of no discernible use to anyone here. A huge sofa upholstered in oilcloth. On the left, a door leading to the interior of the house; on the right, a door to the porch. In front of this righthand door a mat has been laid to prevent the peasants dirtying the floor. Autumn evening. Silence.*

TELEGIN *and* MARINA *sit facing each other, winding stocking wool.*

TELEGIN. Quick, now, or they'll be calling us to say goodbye. They've ordered the horses already.

MARINA (*trying to wind faster*). Only a little bit left.

TELEGIN. They're off to Kharkov. That's where they're going to live.

MARINA. Better so.

TELEGIN. They've taken fright . . . 'Not another hour will I stop in this place,' she says. 'We're leaving, and that's flat . . . We'll put up in Kharkov, and we'll send for our things once we've settled in . . .' They're going with what they stand up in. So there it is – they weren't fated to live here. They just weren't fated to . . . Predestined not to.

MARINA. Better so. All the noise they raised just now, all that shooting – they ought to be ashamed of themselves!

TELEGIN. Yes, it was a regular field of battle.

MARINA. That my eyes should see such things. (*Pause.*) We'll go back to living in the old way, like we did before. Eight o'clock in the morning – tea; one o'clock – dinner; and sit down to supper in the evening; everything in its proper place, the same as in other people's houses . . . like

Christians. (*With a sigh.*) Sinner that I am, it's a long time since I had noodles.

TELEGIN. Yes, it's a long time since they made us noodles. (*Pause.*) A good long time ... I was going through the village this morning and the storekeeper called after me. 'Look at you!' he says. 'Living on their charity!' It left such a bitter taste in my mouth.

MARINA. You pay no heed, my dear. We're all living on the charity of God. You, Sonya, her uncle – we're all the same, we're none of us sitting idle, we're all of us working! Every one of us ... Where is Sonya?

TELEGIN. In the garden. Still going round with the doctor looking for her uncle. They're afraid he might lay hands on himself.

MARINA. Where's his pistol?

TELEGIN (*in a whisper*). I've hidden it in the cellar!

MARINA (*grinning*). Oh, this world of sin!

Enter VANYA *and* ASTROV *from outside.*

VANYA. Leave me alone. (*To* MARINA *and* TELEGIN.) Go away, will you. Let me have a moment to myself! I can't bear being watched over.

TELEGIN. We're going, Vanya, we're going.

TELEGIN *tiptoes out.*

MARINA. You old goose, you!

She makes a cackling noise at VANYA, *then gathers up her wool and goes out.*

VANYA. Leave me alone!

ASTROV. With the greatest of pleasure – I should have been on my way a long time ago. But let me say it again – I am not leaving until you give me back what you've taken from me.

VANYA. I haven't taken anything from you.

ASTROV. I'm serious, now. Don't waste my time. I'm late enough as it is.

VANYA. I haven't taken anything.

They both sit down.

ASTROV. No? All right, I'll give you a little longer, and then I'm sorry, but I shall have to use force. We'll tie you up and search you. Seriously.

VANYA. If you like. (*Pause.*) To be such a fool, though – to shoot twice and miss both times! That's something I shall never forgive myself!

ASTROV. If you wanted to put a bullet in something you might have done better to try your own head.

VANYA (*shrugs*). It's a funny thing. I'm guilty of attempted murder, but no one's arresting me, no one's charging me. So they must think I'm insane. (*Gives a bitter laugh.*) I'm insane, but not people who adopt the mask of a professor, of some learned sage, to conceal their total lack of talent, and their dullness, and their utter callousness. They're not insane. Nor are people who marry old men and then publicly deceive them. I saw you, I saw you with your arms round her!

ASTROV. Yes, sir, I had my arms round her, sir, and pooh to you. (*He thumbs his nose.*)

VANYA (*looking at the door*). No, but it's an insane world, if you people are still part of it.

ASTROV. And that's another stupid remark.

VANYA. So what? I'm insane, I'm not responsible for my actions – I have the right to make stupid remarks.

ASTROV. The joke's worn thin. You're not insane, you're just someone who's got a bit odd. You're a buffoon. There was a time when I had the same idea – that being odd must be sick, must be abnormal. But I've come round to the view now that oddity is the normal condition of mankind. You're entirely normal.

VANYA (*covers his face with his hands*). I'm so ashamed! If you knew how ashamed I felt! There's no pain in the world to compare with these pangs of shame. (*In anguish.*) Unendurable! (*Bends his head low over the table.*) What can I do? What can I do?

ASTROV. Nothing.

VANYA. Give me something to take! Oh, God in heaven ... I'm forty-seven years old; suppose I live to be sixty, then I've still got another thirteen years to go. It's a long time! How am I to get through these thirteen years? What am I going to be doing, what am I going to occupy them with? Oh, imagine, though ...

Convulsively squeezes ASTROV's *hand.*

Just imagine, if one could somehow live the rest of one's life differently. If one could wake up some clear, quiet morning and feel that one had begun life afresh, that the past was all forgotten, had dissolved like smoke. (*Weeps.*) If one could begin a new life ... Give me some idea how to do it ... where to begin ...

ASTROV (*with irritation*). Oh, come on, now! What's all this about a new life? Our situation, yours and mine, is hopeless.

VANYA. Is it?

ASTROV. I'm sure it is.

VANYA. Give me something ... (*Indicating his heart.*) I've got a burning pain here.

ASTROV (*cries out angrily*). Oh, stop it! (*Relenting.*) People living a century or two after we're gone, who'll despise us for leading such stupid and tasteless lives – they may find a way to be happy, but as for us ... There's only one hope left for you and me – that when we're lying in our graves we might have pleasant dreams. (*Sighs.*) Yes, my friend. In the whole district there were only two people of any substance and any culture – you and me. But in ten years or so this narrow provincial life, this despicable life, has dragged us under. Its rotten exhalations have poisoned our blood, and we have become as vile as all the others. (*Sharply.*) But you won't talk me out of it, though. You give me back what you've taken from me.

VANYA. I haven't taken anything from you.

ASTROV. You've taken a bottle of morphine out of my medicine chest. (*Pause.*) Listen, if you absolutely insist upon putting an end to it all then go into the forest and shoot yourself. Give me back the morphine, though, or else people will talk – they'll jump to conclusions and think I gave it to you . . . It's going to be quite bad enough having to do the post mortem. You think that'll be fun?

Enter SONYA.

VANYA. Leave me alone.

ASTROV (*to* SONYA). Your uncle has purloined a bottle of morphine out of my medicine chest and he won't give it back. Tell him, will you, that it's . . . well, not very clever. Also I'm pressed for time. I should be on my way.

SONYA. Uncle Vanya, did you take the morphine?

Pause.

ASTROV. He did. I know he did.

SONYA. Give it back. Why are you trying to frighten us? (*Gently.*) Give it back, Uncle Vanya! I may be just as unhappy as you, but I'm not giving way to despair. I'm enduring it, and I shall go on enduring until my life comes to its natural end . . . You endure as well. (*Pause.*) Give it back!

Kisses his hands.

Dear Uncle, dear sweet kind Uncle, give it back! (*Weeps.*) You're a good man, you must have pity on us and give it back. Endure, Uncle! Endure!

VANYA *gets the bottle out of the table and gives it to* ASTROV.

VANYA. Here, take it. (*To* SONYA.) But quickly now, work, something to do, otherwise I can't go on . . . I just can't go on . . .

SONYA. Yes, yes, work. Just as soon as we've seen everyone off we'll sit down to work . . . (*Sorts agitatedly through the papers on the table.*) We're so behind with everything . . .

ASTROV (*puts the bottle in his medicine chest, which he then straps up*). Now I can be off, then.

Enter YELENA.

YELENA. Vanya? We'll be leaving in a moment . . . Go and see my husband – he's got something to say to you.

SONYA. Do go, Uncle Vanya. (*Takes* VANYA *by the arm.*) We'll both go. You and Papa must make it up. You absolutely must.

Exeunt SONYA *and* VANYA.

YELENA. I'm leaving.

Gives ASTROV *her hand.*

Goodbye.

ASTROV. So soon?

YELENA. They've brought the horses.

ASTROV. Goodbye, then.

YELENA. A little while ago you promised me you'd leave.

ASTROV. I haven't forgotten. I am just leaving. (*Pause.*) You've taken fright? (*Takes her hand.*) Is this really so dreadful?

YELENA. Yes.

ASTROV. You could stay, though! Yes? Tomorrow, in the forest . . .

YELENA. No . . . It's been decided . . . That's precisely why I'm facing you so bravely – because it's been decided that we're leaving . . . I'm going to ask one thing of you – to think better of me. I should like you to have some respect for me.

ASTROV. Oh . . . (*He makes a gesture of impatience.*) Please stay. Admit it, now – you've nothing in the world to do, no aim in life, nothing to occupy your attention, and you're going to give way to your feelings sooner or later – it's inevitable. Better, surely, if it's not in Kharkov or Kursk, but here in the bosom of nature . . . Poetic, at least – it's beautiful even in autumn . . . You've got the forest, you've got decayed estates *à la* Turgenev.

YELENA. What an absurd man you are . . . I'm angry with you, but all the same . . . I shall remember you with pleasure. You're an interesting and unusual person. We shall never see each other again, so why try to hide it? I was, yes, a little carried away by you. So, let's shake hands and part friends. Remember me kindly.

ASTROV (*shaking hands*). Yes, off you go, then . . . (*Reflectively.*) You seem in fact to be a good and sincere person; but there also seems to be something curious about your whole way of being. Here was everyone working away, going about their business, creating something – and as soon as you and your husband arrived they had to drop it all and spend the whole summer worrying about nothing but his gout and you. The pair of you infected us all with your idleness. I got carried away – I've done nothing for a whole month, while people have been falling sick and peasants have been pasturing their cattle in my woods and plantations . . . So, you see, you and your husband sow destruction wherever you go . . . I'm joking, of course, but all the same it is . . . odd, and I'm sure that had you stayed there would have been devastation on the most colossal scale. I should have been done for, and the outlook for you would have been . . . less than bright. So, off you go, then. *Finita la commedia!*

YELENA (*takes a pencil off his table and quickly hides it away*). I'll take this pencil to remember you by.

ASTROV. It is curious, though, isn't it . . . To have known each other and now suddenly for some reason never to see each other again. It's the same with everything in this world . . . Before anyone comes, until Uncle Vanya walks in with a bouquet, will you allow me to . . . kiss you . . . Kiss you goodbye . . . Yes?

Kisses her cheek.

So . . . There we are, then.

YELENA. I should like to wish you all the best. (*Looks round.*) Oh, hang it all – just for once in my life!

She embraces him abruptly, and then they both at once move quickly apart.

I must go.

ASTROV. Go quickly. If the horses are here you can start.

YELENA. I think people are coming.

They both listen.

ASTROV. *Finita!*

Enter SEREBRYAKOV, VANYA, MARIA VASILYEVNA *with
a book,* TELEGIN, *and* SONYA.

SEREBRYAKOV (*to* VANYA). Dead and buried, then, the whole
thing, and let it so remain. Since it happened, in these few
short hours, I have gone over so much and so much in my
mind that I believe I could write a complete treatise for
future generations on how to live one's life. I gladly accept
your apologies and ask you to accept mine. Goodbye, then.

He and VANYA *kiss three times.*

VANYA. You'll get precisely what you got before. Everything
will be as it was.

YELENA *embraces* SONYA. SEREBRYAKOV *kisses* MARIA
VASILYEVNA's *hand.*

SEREBRYAKOV. *Maman* . . .

MARIA VASILYEVNA *kisses him.*

MARIA VASILYEVNA. Alexandre, have your photograph taken
again and send me a copy. You know how dear you are to
me.

TELEGIN. Goodbye, Professor! Don't forget us, now!

SEREBRYAKOV *kisses his daughter.*

SEREBRYAKOV. Goodbye, my dear . . . Goodbye to everyone.

Gives his hand to ASTROV.

Thank you for the pleasure of your company . . . I respect
your way of thinking, I respect your impulsiveness and your
enthusiasm, but permit an old man to make one parting
observation: get down to the practicalities, ladies and
gentlemen! Get down to practicalities!

General farewells.

My best wishes to you all!

Exit SEREBRYAKOV, *followed by* MARIA VASILYEVNA
and SONYA. VANYA *firmly kisses* YELENA's *hand.*

VANYA. Goodbye ... Forgive me ... We shall never see each other again.

YELENA (*moved*). Goodbye, my dear.

Kisses him on the head, and goes out.

ASTROV (*to* TELEGIN). Ilyusha, tell them they might as well bring my horses at the same time.

TELEGIN. I'll tell them.

Exit TELEGIN. ASTROV *and* VANYA *are left on their own.* ASTROV *clears his paints off the table and puts them away in his suitcase.*

ASTROV. Why don't you go and see them off?

VANYA. Let them go – I just ... haven't the heart. I'm so wretched. Quickly, I must get myself occupied with something. Work, work! (*Rummages among the papers on the table.*)

Pause. There is the sound of harness-bells.

ASTROV. They've gone. The professor's pleased, I should imagine. You wouldn't get him back now for all the tea in China.

Enter MARINA.

MARINA. They've gone. (*Sits down in the armchair and winds wool.*)

Enter SONYA.

SONYA. They've gone. (*Wipes her eyes.*) Please God everything's all right. (*To her uncle.*) So, let's do something, Uncle Vanya.

VANYA. Work, work ...

SONYA. A long, long time since we last sat together at this table. (*Lights the lamp on the table.*) No ink, by the look of it ... (*Takes the inkwell across to the cupboard and refills it.*) I'm sad they've gone.

MARIA VASILYEVNA *comes slowly in.*

MARIA VASILYEVNA. They've gone! (*Sits down and immerses herself in her reading.*)

SONYA (*sits at the table and leafs through an account-book*). Uncle Vanya, let's start by writing out the accounts. We're terribly behind. There were people sending round a second time for their accounts today. Go on, then. You do one, I'll do the next . . .

VANYA (*writes*). 'Invoice . . . '

They both write in silence.

MARINA (*yawns*). I could just drop off now . . .

ASTROV. Silence. The scratching of pens, the chirp of the cricket. All warm and snug . . . I don't feel much like leaving.

The sound of harness-bells.

They're bringing the horses . . . I suppose it only remains to say goodbye to you, my friends, and goodbye to my table, and then – off I go! (*Puts the maps away in the portfolio.*)

MARINA. Why all the hustle and bustle? Stay here, why not?

ASTROV. I mustn't.

VANYA (*writes*). 'Balance outstanding – two hundred and seventy-five rubles . . .'

Enter the WORKMAN.

WORKMAN (*to* ASTROV). The horses are here.

ASTROV. Right.

Gives him the medicine-chest, the suitcase, and the portfolio.

Here, take these. Mind you don't buckle the portfolio.

WORKMAN. Sir.

Exit the WORKMAN.

ASTROV. Well, then . . . (*Goes to make his farewells.*)

SONYA. When shall we see you again?

ASTROV. Not before next summer, I suppose. Scarcely in the winter . . . Of course, in an emergency just let me know and I'll come over.

Shakes people's hands.

Thank you for having me here, and for all your kindness . . . well, for everything.

Goes across to MARINA *and kisses her on the head.*

Goodbye, Nanna.

MARINA. You won't have a glass of tea before you go?

ASTROV. I won't, Nanna.

MARINA. A drop of vodka, perhaps?

ASTROV (*irresolutely*). Well . . .

Exit MARINA. *Pause.*

One of my horses is running a little lame. I noticed it yesterday, when he was taken to be watered.

VANYA. He'll need to be re-shod.

ASTROV. I'll have to look in at the blacksmith's. No help for it. (*Goes over to the map of Africa and looks at it.*) While out in Africa here the heat must be terrible now!

VANYA. Yes, probably.

MARINA *returns carrying a tray with a glass of vodka and a piece of bread on it.*

MARINA. Here you are.

ASTROV *drinks the vodka.*

Good health to you, my dear. (*Bows low.*) You should have a morsel of bread with it, though.

ASTROV. No, just like that . . . So, all the best! (*To* MARINA.) No need to see me out, Nanna.

Exit ASTROV. SONYA *goes after him with a candle to show him out.* MARINA *sits down in her armchair.*

VANYA (*writes*). 'Second of February – twenty pounds of sunflower oil . . . Sixteenth of February – another twenty pounds of sunflower oil . . . Buckwheat . . .'

Pause. The sound of harness-bells.

MARINA. He's gone.

Pause. SONYA *returns, and puts the candle on the table.*

SONYA. He's gone . . .

VANYA (*calculates on the abacus and writes*). In total . . . fifteen . . . twenty-five . . .

SONYA *sits down and writes.*

MARINA (*yawns*). Oh, sinners that we are . . .

Enter TELEGIN *on tiptoe. He sits down by the door and quietly strums his guitar.* VANYA *strokes* SONYA's *hair.*

VANYA. Oh, my child, I'm so wretched! If you only knew how wretched I was!

SONYA. What can we do, though? We must live our lives! (*Pause.*) We shall live our lives, Uncle Vanya. We shall live out the long, long succession of days and endless evenings; we shall patiently bear the trials we're sent; we shall labour for others from now into our old age without respite; and when our time comes we shall die with resignation; and there, beyond the grave, we shall say that we have suffered and wept, that it went hard with us; and God will be moved to pity; and you and I, Uncle, dear Uncle, shall see a life of light and beauty and grace; and we shall rejoice; and we shall look back on the unhappiness of this present time with tenderness, with a smile – and we shall rest. I have faith, Uncle, I have a burning and passionate faith . . .

Kneels before him and lays her head upon his hands.

(*Wearily.*) We shall rest!

TELEGIN *quietly plays his guitar.*

We shall rest! We shall hear the angels; we shall see the sky all dressed in diamonds; we shall see all this world's evil and all our sufferings drown in the mercy that will fill the earth; and our life will become as quiet and gentle and sweet as a caress. I have faith, I have faith . . .

Wipes away his tears with her handkerchief.

Poor Uncle Vanya, poor Uncle Vanya, you're crying . . . (*On the verge of tears herself.*) You've never known joy in all your life, but you wait, Uncle Vanya, you wait . . . We shall rest . . .

Embraces him.

We shall rest!

The sound of the WATCHMAN *knocking.* TELEGIN *quietly strums his guitar;* MARIA VASILYEVNA *writes in the margins of her pamphlet;* MARINA *winds her wool.*

We shall rest!

The curtain slowly falls.

Notes

title page: the sub-title of the original is 'Scenes from country
life in four acts'. *The Wood Demon* was described as 'A
comedy in four acts'. Although it is not indicated by Chekhov,
Donald Rayfield seems clear about where *The Wood Demon*
and *Uncle Vanya* are located. In the latter play, 'Chekhov has
moved his action two hundred miles east, from the idyllic well-
watered countryside of the north-east Ukraine to a tired and
over-populated central Russian landscape somewhere on the
railway-line between Serpukhov and Kharkov' (Rayfield, 1995,
p.42).

2 *Serebryakov, professor emeritus*: 'Aleksandr Vladimirovich
Serebryakov, a retired professor' in the original. A professor
'emeritus' is an honorary distinction conferred on someone with
a distinguished academic career who no longer occupies a
university chair. A source for the character might be one M.O.
Menshikov, who visited Melikhovo in August 1896 and
inspired the following entry in Chekhov's notebook: 'M. in dry
weather walks about in galoshes, carries an umbrella, in order
not to perish from sunstroke, he is frightened of washing in
cold water, and complains of his heart missing a beat' (Peace,
1983, p.61).

Yelena: critics have pointed out that the root of her name *len'*
suggests 'laziness'. In *The Wood Demon* she is compared to
Homer's Helen of Troy but critics believe the more appropriate
comparison in *Uncle Vanya* should be with the more parodical
Helen of Offenbach's operetta on the same theme, *La Belle
Hélène*.

Sonya: Sonya is a derivative of Sofia.

Maria Vasilyevna: described as the 'widow of a privy
councillor' in the original, i.e. she was married to someone
who held a post at court.

Vanya: 'Ivan Petrovich Voinitsky' in the original.

Astrov: the name may be derived from the Latin *astrum* (a
star). In Act Two, Serebryakov states his belief that Astrov

knows as much about medicine as he (the professor) knows
about astronomy.

Telegin: see A Note on the Translation, p. lxxxvi.

Marina, the old nurse: the 'niania', or 'nianka' (nanny), had a
very special place in aristocratic homes. Of peasant origin, she
would often act as surrogate parent and exercise a powerful
influence over her upper-class infant charges as well as
occupying a strong place in their affections. It was not unusual
for the 'niania' to live on in the family home long after the
children had grown up.

Watchman: not mentioned in Chekhov's own cast list. His is
an off-stage role.

Act One

3 *samovar*: a tea urn containing water heated with charcoal from
which a teapot placed on top can constantly be replenished.

a glass of tea: Russians frequently drink tea from a glass rather
than a cup, the hot receptacle being placed in a metal holder
with a drinking handle.

Sonya's mother: she is referred to as 'Vera Petrovna' in the
original and is something of a mystery figure. She (and
presumably her husband) appear to have spent two winters in
the countryside which the professor declares he despises even in
the summer months. Do the doctor's visits during two winters
mean that she was ill during that period? Or was there a love
interest which Astrov is now redirecting towards Yelena?

You were a young man then: Yelena later says that Astrov
looks as though he's in his late thirties. If she is right, then
Astrov would have been about twenty-six at the time.

go to bed and lie there just waiting: the image is that of a
frightened little boy hiding under the covers scared of being
dragged away, rather than a doctor waiting to attend a patient.

It drags its feet, this life of ours: the kind of complaint which
characters in the play frequently make as if to suggest that an
early death, or a speedier journey to the grave, might be
preferable to prolonging life's agony.

cranks and crackbrains: the Russian for both is 'chudaki'
(eccentrics or abnormal types) and is a running refrain.

4 *You want something to eat perhaps?*: when offering Astrov tea,
and now something to eat, Marina uses the verb 'kushat',

rather than 'est'; the former would more usually be used when addressing a child.

Lent: the period of forty days, from Ash Wednesday to Easter Saturday, kept as a time of fasting and penitence in commemoration of Christ's fasting in the wilderness.

Typhus: a fever spread by rat fleas. Epidemics were common among the peasantry in nineteenth-century Russia because of the over-crowded living conditions. As a doctor himself, Chekhov would have been very familiar with them.

a shunter: an engine driver who works in a marshalling yard shunting freight cars. Presumably he has had an accident at work necessitating an operation.

chloroform: a thin colourless liquid, smelling of ether which, when inhaled, produces insensibility. It was used as an anaesthetic and could be fatal in excessive amounts or if inhaled by someone already enfeebled by loss of blood, as may have been the case here. It is typical that Astrov should think of this incident egocentrically (there is no reason why he should feel guilty) instead of thinking of the objective tragedy of the man's death and its likely financial effect on his family.

I sat down and I closed my eyes . . . The people who come after us: a fairly pointless speculation in the circumstances when the need is to worry about what happens here and now. Vershinin in Chekhov's *Three Sisters* engages in similarly self-indulgent speculation.

Thank you. Well said: there is a good deal of emphasis in the play on the capacity to speak effectively rather than do anything.

straightens his stylish tie: a somewhat superfluous adornment, given Vanya's otherwise rumpled appearance and his country surroundings. Perhaps it is a concession to civilised 'city' values or something worn for Yelena's sake. Whatever the case, the *absence* of a tie, especially in the presence of the opposite sex, is something which also affects Astrov's behaviour later (see p.22).

5 *Vanya (whistles)*: when indicating to Stanislavsky the difference between Astrov and Vanya, Chekhov explained that Astrov whistled whereas Vanya wept.

The professor has decided he is going to live here: we later learn that the professor cannot stand living in the country and plans to sell the estate.

Quite remarkable, Professor: in the original, Telegin addresses
the professor rather formally as 'Your Excellency'. Being a
retired professor, Serebryakov has attained the highest rank in
the Russian Civil Service which is equivalent to that of an
army major-general and entitles him to be addressed as 'Your
Excellency'.

Papa: note how economically Chekhov establishes the
relationship between father and daughter; Sonya addresses him
twice between entry and exit and is ignored on both occasions.

umbrella . . . overcoat, gloves, and galoshes: critics have
pointed to comparisons between this description of Serebryakov
and the central character of Chekhov's short story, 'The Man
in a Case'.

6 *the dawn of a new life*: rather like Mrs Alving in Ibsen's
Ghosts, Vanya's mother seems to be interested in radical ideas
which were circulating in European society at the end of the
nineteenth century. There is a suggestion that Serebryakov is
also something of a radical thinker which is, perhaps, why she
admires her son-in-law.

sits writing in his study: in the original, Vanya quotes from a
satire of 1794 by I.I. Dmitriev (see A Note on the Translation,
p. lxxxvi).

sacristan: a church sexton, who has responsibility for care of
the church building and contents as well as preparation for
burials.

a seminary: a school or college for training men for the
priesthood.

he got a chair: he was made a university professor. Presumably,
Serebryakov abandoned the priesthood for the humanities.

son-in-law of a senator: a member of the Senate would have
ranked high in the Russian Civil Service – higher than a
general in the military.

realism and naturalism: precise distinctions between the two
genres are difficult to define. The naturalist movement,
influenced by the evolutionary ideas of Darwin and
philosophical notions of materialist determinism (see p. xix),
was at its height during the final twenty years or so of the
nineteenth century. Typical representatives were the French
novelist Emile Zola and middle-period Ibsen. The naturalist
movement in painting can be traced back to the eighteenth
century and, in particular, to the work of Dutch still-life
painters.

7 *and not a soul has ever heard of him*: this belief appears to be unfounded based on what Yelena says later (p. 28). In *The Wood Demon*, Khrushchev makes it plain that Serebryakov is a well-known and respected figure in the wider world.

Don Juan: the prototype of the conscienceless libertine made famous by the Spanish Renaissance dramatist Tirso de Molina, the French dramatist Molière, the English poet Byron and, especially, by Mozart in his opera *Don Giovanni*.

She loved him the way only the angels can: based on what he goes on to say, Vanya seems, without realising it, to be identifying Serebryakov as someone 'as fine and pure' as his sister. Some critics have made a good deal of the absent sister/ mother/wife, even going so far as to suggest that the play is about losing her and a consequent loss of faith. Her name, Vera, means 'faith' in Russian.

8 *Sonya (to Marina hurriedly)*: presumably, Sonya has come on stage specifically to ask Marina to deal with the peasants, which may be because she feels uneasy with them for some reason, is possibly even frightened of them or feels Marina will deal with them better.

Meanwhile I've come galloping eighteen miles: this looks like a complaint but Astrov, it seems, is only too willing to abandon his real work as a doctor to attend to Serebryakov as it brings him into contact with Yelena. He would not have ridden his own horse but driven, or been driven, in a carriage of some sort.

No, ma'am: in the original Astrov says. 'Net-s', the 's' being a contraction of 'sudarnia', an old-fashioned way a subordinate would address a superior. Astrov is being playful rather than ironic.

9 *Kharkov*: the second largest city in the Ukraine situated to the south-east of Kiev (Ukraine's capital) and some 600 miles south-west of Moscow.

maman: in French in the original. The Russian upper classes tended to speak as readily in French as Russian during the nineteenth century. The opening conversation of Tolstoy's *War and Peace* is actually written in French. Maria Vasilyevna calls Vanya 'Jean'.

because of my age!: the absurdity of Vanya's feeling that he cannot achieve anything in life because he's reached the ripe old age of forty-seven should be obvious.

Uncle Vanya: this is the first time that the play's title has been
used as a form of address and a reminder that Vanya is 'uncle'
to only one person in the play.

You should have got down to business: Maria Vasilyevna uses
an expression which she has presumably heard from
Serebryakov's lips (unless he has heard it from hers) as he
repeats it in Act Four, 'Nuzhno bylo delo delat', which is
usually translated as 'You should get down to work', but is
more like 'You should be up and doing'. Commentators have
noted the similarity between this slogan and the title of a
radically progressive novel by the proto-revolutionary
philosopher, Nikolai Chernyshevski, *Chto delat?* (*What is to be
Done?*, 1863), which so inspired Lenin that he gave his own
political programme the same title in 1911. When Serebryakov
repeats the phrase in Act Four, it is translated as 'get down to
practicalities'.

10 *Cheep, cheep, cheep*: in *Three Sisters*, the disturbing figure of
Soleny directs these same sounds, as a comment on his
meaningless chatter, at Tusenbach whom he later kills in a
duel. Chekhov could here be using Marina as a vehicle to
comment on the meaningless babble of the disputants. 'I don't
want the crows getting them' may have similar associations to
those evoked in *The Wood Demon* where, as Donald Rayfield
suggests, 'when Iulia constantly worries about her turkey chicks
and Fiodor Orlovsky suddenly drinks to a passing hawk, the
summery outdoor mood is darkened by imagery of prey and
predator' (Rayfield, 1995, p.20).

that piece of waste ground: this phrase has been grist to the
mill of those critics who interpret the play in terms of 'waste' –
wasted lives, wasted opportunities, wasted time. In post-
emancipation Russia, peasants could lease plots of land from
their former masters for their own cultivation even if, or
especially if, as seems the case here, the land itself was of poor
quality.

No, it'll be too late by that time: this line is followed in the
original by his looking for his cap muttering: 'Where on earth
. . . Where's it got to . . . ' which he repeats after the workman
exits (see A Note on the Translation, p. lxxxv). The fact that
the workman has travelled all this way suggests an emergency,
but it is noticeable that Astrov is more concerned about finding
his cap than finding out why he has been called away.

In some play by Ostrovsky: Aleksandr Ostrovsky (1823–86) is considered to be Russia's greatest, and certainly most prolific, playwright (see A Note on the Translation, p.lxxxv).

11 *a bronze medal*: it may be significant that the medal is neither silver nor gold.

forests: for the importance of Chekhov's views on ecology see Simon Karlinsky's essay 'Huntsmen, Birds, Forests, and Three Sisters' in Barricelli, 1981, pp.144–60.

12 *if a thousand years from now*: this all seems very modern but Chekhov was familiar with the work of Russian writers on climate (dating from the 1880s) and, specifically, an essay of 1878 on 'The Influence of Forests on the Climate' by Aleksandr Voieikov. Astrov, like Vershinin in *Three Sisters* tends to indulge in time spans of hundreds and thousands of years. It is interesting to note that he speaks of his 'guilt' for people being happy *in the future* – 'a tiny bit my fault'. Is Chekhov perhaps implying that happiness *now* is what he, and we, should be concerned with?

13 *Did you have to annoy your mother . . . ?*: noticeably she does not suggest that she herself was annoyed by the insult to her husband.

there will be neither faithfulness nor innocence left in the world, nor any capacity for self-sacrifice: Yelena purports to be speaking in general terms; in fact, she can be seen to be speaking about herself and her own marriage.

she's in love with him and I can see why. He's been here three times already since I arrived: notice how the speech seems to be concerned with her perception of the feelings of Sonya for Astrov but slips into a subconscious recognition of her perception of Astrov's feelings for herself.

an evil woman: 'chto ia zla' doesn't necessarily imply evil but 'hostile' in the sense of not liking other people and possibly capable of hurting them.

14 *just let me look at you . . . Let me talk about my love*: there is a strong suggestion that this is all Vanya is capable of – i.e. looking and talking; action is beyond him.

Telegin strikes the strings . . . Maria Vasilyevna makes a note: the stage direction anticipates a similar one at the final curtain of Act Four as the action of the play appears to come full circle to a static and repetitive conclusion.

Act Two

15 *The Watchman can be heard knocking*: this stage direction is
interpreted in several, often contradictory, ways from a sound
made by beating an iron rail to the kind of noise made by a
football fan's rattle. Paul Schmidt explains: 'The tapping sound,
made by a hand-held wooden device with a large clapper, is
hollow, rather like a gavel on wood, probably in a pattern of
two strokes in two seconds, then a pause of five or six seconds,
then a repetition' (*The Plays of Anton Chekhov*, trans. Paul
Schmidt, New York, HarperCollins, 1997, p.254). The
watchman was employed to patrol the grounds of, especially
isolated, estates to warn off thieves and ne'er-do-wells.

Oh, you . . . : in the original, Serebryakov says, 'You,
Lenochka . . .', using the intimate form of her name which is
appropriate between husband and wife, or for an older person
addressing a younger. It is the only time in the course of the
play that this form of her name is used.

I'm stifling: critics have drawn attention to the symbolic
importance of weather conditions in the play as a kind of
metaphor for the human condition. It is sultry and overcast in
Acts One and Two, then a storm breaks literally and
metaphorically in Acts Two and Three, after which people are
able to breathe more easily.

gout . . . rheumatism: they are both physical complaints,
usually accompanied by swelling, which affect the smaller
joints, the former the feet and the latter the whole body.

a complete Batyushkov: the poems of Konstantin Batyushkov
(1787–1855) which attracted the praise of Pushkin.

Turgenev: Ivan Sergeevich Turgenev (1818–83), Russian
novelist and dramatist.

angina: a dangerous heart condition of which the symptoms are
violent chest pains.

16 *you want to live your life*: a constant theme of the play – the
desire to live but also the fear of life, or a sense of life as
something to be endured rather than lived to the full.

that old idiot of a mother of his: his mother-in-law would be
devastated if she knew the opinion held of her by her revered
son-in-law.

The window bangs in the wind: Donald Rayfield attributes
sinister import to this stage direction: 'The unseen outside
world, with the ominous noise of the guard striking his

wooden board and the window banging in the wind, operates
on the audience with a mix of the comic and horrific'
(Rayfield, 1995, p.20).

17 *I want to live . . . I like being well-known*: the theme is
repeated. The second phrase also suggests that, contrary to
Vanya's earlier assertion, the professor has a worthwhile
academic reputation and is not totally unknown.
in Siberia: Siberia is the remote area of Russia to which
criminals and political rebels were traditionally sent to serve
terms of hard labour in the salt mines.
in five or six years I shall be old as well: she'll be thirty-two
or, at most, thirty-three.
holy fool: a 'iurodivy', a peculiarly Russian type of the saintly
madman who frequently makes an appearance in Russian
literature and who illustrates God's compassion for the afflicted
by His endowing them with a divine spark. Here, Serebryakov
is referring ironically to Astrov's ecological enthusiasms.
I've got the haymaking: it is already clear that a storm is likely
and rain-soaked hay cannot be gathered. It also becomes clear
that Sonya already knows that the hay has lain rotting in the
fields for weeks (p.22).

18 *couldn't sleep at night for grieving*: another aspect of the
mystery surrounding Vera Petrovna, what was she grieving
about? As Marina continues, Vera's symptoms sound like those
of depression. Some critics have even gone so far as to suggest
that the professor's first wife may have committed suicide.
Kisses Serebryakov's shoulder: a Russian form of salutation
offered by inferiors to their superiors.
lime tea: tea made from the flowers of the lime tree and
possessing soothing properties.

19 Throughout this scene Vanya and Yelena address each other by
the formal 'vy' instead of the more intimate 'ty'.
a demon: 'domovoi' literally a 'house goblin'.
my life is lost beyond recall: although purporting to dislike
philosophising, Vanya is prone to philosophise at length during
this scene about his and Yelena's wasted lives, culminating in
the less than profound observation that 'All things are
possible!'

20 *She's gone . . .*: the following soliloquy seems slightly unnatural
in a predominantly realistic play. Chekhov perhaps simply
recognises that it is a dramatic convention, although he

dispenses with soliloquies in his final two plays.

I used to meet her at my sister's: another mystery. What was Yelena's relationship with her husband's first wife? That of a friend?

'Don't be afraid, I'm here': the image is of father and child rather than husband and wife, or 'babes in the wood'.

I've been so duped: Vanya's change of heart does not seem to be based objectively on the calibre of the professor's work but subjectively on his personal feelings about the man himself.

21 *Enter Astrov in a frock coat*: why the formal attire? It seems as incongruous in this setting as Vanya's elegant tie but may also be inspired by the presence of Yelena.

(*Puts his hands on his hips and sings quietly*): the gesture of hands on hips suggests that this is a dance as well as a song. In the original, Astrov sings a folk song: 'Khodi khata, khodi pech', khoziainu negde lech' . . .' ('Move, hut, move stove, the master has no room to lie down') (see A Note on the Translation, p. lxxxvi). According to Donald Rayfield, 'Any Russian audience knows that the song then moves to ribaldry' (Rayfield, 1995, p.48).

Tula: an industrial town about one hundred miles south of Moscow and made famous by Nikolai Leskov in his short story *The Tale of the Left-Handed Craftsman from Tula and the Steel Flea* (1881).

22 *a rather vile sort of man*: a 'poshliak' in the original, derived from the noun 'poshlost', a term normally associated with the literary world of Gogol and implying a mixture of the banal, the vulgar and the kitsch. We can take it that Astrov's self-accusal is, simultaneously, a form of self-exoneration.

I take on the trickiest operations . . . just microbes: the view we get of Astrov when drunk is, we assume, not one Sonya would approve of, or Yelena, for all their expressed admiration for the man. He would certainly run the risk of being dismissed from his post for performing operations in an intoxicated state.

Sees Sonya entering: there is a missing line before Sonya's entry in which Astrov refers to the way in which his assistant pronounces the third person singular of the verb 'to go' (idet) as if it were 'idiot', for which it is hard to find an English equivalent. A variant might be: 'All right? There's an assistant of mine who never says 'All right' but 'All white'. He's a terrible swindler. So, then, all white?' (see A Note on the Translation, p. lxxxvi).

estate work: some critics have identified 'work' as a key theme in the play. Chekhov certainly seems interested in what constitutes work and who does it (see Translator's Introduction, p. lxxvii–lxxix).

23 *You looked at me just then like your poor dead mother*: it may be significant that the resemblance is noted while Sonya is admonishing Vanya and complaining of being overworked.

Known what? . . . never mind . . . Later: yet another mystery surrounding the dead sister. Is this an indication of something, or nothing?

We'll drink no more: Sonya is encouraging Astrov to abstain from vodka, rather than wine; the effect of it is more addictive and pernicious. By Act Four, the pledge has been broken.

24 *Uncle Vanya and his gloom*: the fact that Astrov calls him 'Uncle Vanya' rather than 'Ivan Petrovich' suggests he is mocking or patronising him. He later warns Yelena that 'Uncle Vanya might come in', just before they embrace in Act Four, ironically recalling his interruption of their earlier embrace in Act Three.

Would the mirror on her wall . . .: see A Note on the Translation, p. lxxxv. Astrov is quoting from Pushkin's allusion to the beautiful but destructive stepmother of the Snow White tale: 'She is beautiful, there's no denying that' (Ona prekrasna, spora net), cf. Peace, 1983, p.62.

I work . . . harder than anyone in the district: we have to take his word for it.

no gleam of light in the distance: the sentiments of a bachelor doomed to return to a dark and empty house. In Yefremov's Moscow Art Theatre production, seen in London in 1989, this became a symbolic light of hope which was left gleaming in the dark at the end of a production which, otherwise, concluded on a note of despair.

25 *preoccupied with analysis and introspection*: you might say that Astrov both is and is not preoccupied with these things, otherwise he would not be so insensitive as to tell Sonya to her face that he loves no one.

what label to stick on me: Astrov starts by generalising, but it emerges that he is talking about himself. In Act Four he declares that he and Vanya are the only educated people in the province (p.51).

why do you want to be like ordinary people ... *?*: it is clear
from what he's been saying that Astrov does not think he *is*
like ordinary people.

Basta!: Italian in the original, 'Enough!'.

as long as I live (Looks at his watch): an ironic moment of
Chekhovian juxtaposition!

Let's go on with our conversation: hardly a conversation, more
a one-sided peroration.

I've had my day, my time is past ...: Yelena says he is thirty-
six or seven.

There's no one I love: Astrov has mentioned this fact so many
times it would seem he is rather proud of the fact.

26 *one of my patients died under the chloroform*: Astrov is
repeating more or less what he has told Marina at the
beginning of Act One. In many respects, Astrov can be seen as
a forerunner of Vershinin in *Three Sisters* in his harping on his
own misfortunes whenever a sympathetic female ear is
available.

other things to think about ... *I must go*: is Astrov being
crassly insensitive in failing to understand Sonya or is he
simply being cruel?

Sonya (alone): again the device of the soliloquy seems a trifle
strained but it allows the audience to perceive Sonya as a
decent, romantic, and very naive individual with a conventional
sense of what it means to be beautiful. It also lets us know
that she is a churchgoer with a religious sensibility and so
prepares an audience for her final soliloquy in Act Four. We
can assume that the church serves a local village so we also
know that the estate is perhaps not so isolated as it otherwise
seems.

27 *Gone*: anticipates the repetitions of the same word in the finale
to Act Four.

Sonya!: in the original, Yelena addresses her by the more
familiar variant of her name, 'Sophie', as a prelude to her
friendly overture.

let's drink to being friends: see A Note on the Translation,
p.lxxxvi. Russians say, as they do here, 'Let's drink to
bruderschaft', using the German term. They then link arms and
drink either from the same glass or from the one each holds in
their own hand.

friends?: in the original they agree to be on 'ty' terms, i.e. to use the 'thou' rather than the 'you' form.

you thought I married your father for his money: there is no suggestion that Sonya has believed this. The tension between the two may simply arise from the fact that they are stepdaughter and stepmother and possibly very much the same age; Sonya may even be the elder.

28 *he was a learned and famous man*: this contradicts Vanya's assertion that Serebryakov is stupid and virtually unknown.

It wasn't real love, it was artificial: not the kind of confession a wife should be making to her husband's daughter, one suspects.

from the very day of our wedding: when was this? Despite the fact that Vanya's sister died some eleven years previously, the professor's remarriage may only be recent and their present extended visit may be the first time that Sonya and her stepmother have spent any time together since the wedding, which may also be contributing to the tension between them.

looking at the dark glass in the window and thinking I can see his face there: logically, if you look through a darkened window all you can see is your own face.

29 *In music, in my husband's house, in all my romances ... a minor character*: the phrase 'in all my romances' (vo vsekh romanakh) also appears in other translations as 'in all my romantic affairs', which is the sense here. However, 'roman' in Russian means 'a novel' as well as 'a romance', so an alternative translation could be 'in all the novels [I read]' (there is no 'my' in the original). In other words, Yelena's view of Astrov and the life he leads is not something she knows anything about from direct experience but has been gleaned from her reading, which her reference to being a 'minor character' (episodicheskoe litso) would seem to substantiate. She does not see herself in the role of the heroine but a character whose life is of little interest.

Hey, boy! Here boy!: in the original the watchman summons his dogs 'Zhuchka' and 'Malchik' (the English would be something like 'Beetle' and 'Boy').

30 *No!*: there is a pointedness in the fact that Yelena's command to Yefim that he make no noise is followed by Serebryakov's similar command to her.

Act Three

31 *Vanya and Sonya, sitting. Yelena, walking*: note how the
    pattern of stasis and movement repeats the opening of Act
    One.

32 *mermaid's blood*: the blood of a 'rusalka' in the original. A
    'rusalka' is the spirit of a river-nymph, usually that of a
    drowned maiden who tempts men to a watery grave.
    Run wild for once in your life: Yelena later soliloquises on this
    theme and may be said to follow Vanya's advice in Act Four,
    but to rather feeble effect when she finally summons up the
    courage to embrace Astrov.
    Autumn roses . . . mournful roses: presumably these should be
    gentle colours rather than passionate red ones as they often are
    in productions.
    He's painting something: in the original 'Chto-to pishet',
    literally 'Writing something', but the present translator has
    chosen to describe him working on his maps.

33 *Let me have a talk to him*: commentators who feel hostile to
    Yelena take this to be part of her plot to woo Astrov in
    Sonya's stead while simultaneously seeking to destroy the
    possibility of any future relationship between her stepdaughter
    and Astrov. She is also seen as a hypocrite, given her high-
    minded speeches about the destructiveness of people.

34 *Yelena (alone)*: yet again, a rather unnatural soliloquy but it
    enables an audience to understand that Yelena appears to be
    acting in good faith.
    Fly off as free as a bird: the bird imagery is stronger in *The
    Wood Demon* where, noticeably, Yelena is described as a tame
    cagebird, a canary. Simon Karlinsky notes: 'The text of *The
    Wood Demon* is permeated by two sets of contrasting bird
    symbols [. . .] Yelena and Sonya are likened to caged captive
    birds [. . .] Serebryakov is compared to a horned owl, and
    Khrushchev promises [. . .] that he will grow the wings of a
    free eagle. [. . .] This avian imagery was eliminated in *Uncle
    Vanya*' ('Huntsmen, Birds, Forest, and Three Sisters' in
    Barricelli, 1981, p.154).

35 *St Petersburg*: Russia's second largest city, after Moscow, built
    during the early eighteenth century on the Gulf of Finland at
    the behest of Tsar Peter I (Peter the Great) as 'a window into
    Europe'.
    At the Conservatoire: this is a music school and the suggestion

is that Yelena was a talented girl who studied the piano from an early age at this prestigious institution which also offered a general education to the privileged few it admitted.

click away on the abacus: doing their financial calculations on a square wooden frame with sliding counters on wire cross-struts. These were still being used in shops and supermarkets in the Soviet Union eighty years later in preference to automatic cash registers.

busy with my colouring: the picture he paints is of a classroom with children doing their sums in one corner and others drawing and colouring in maps.

allow myself this pleasure . . . once a month: does Chekhov impishly imagine he might allow himself a visit to a brothel instead?

36 *little monasteries*: 'hermitages of the Old Believers' in the original – those who fought against changes being introduced into the Russian Orthodox Church during the eighteenth century and who were subject to persecution, even going to the lengths of mass suicide as a gesture of protest.

capercailzies have all vanished: as they had also from the British Isles. A type of large bustard, which used to be found in Scotland. An attempt was made in 2004 to reintroduce the species to the British Isles by releasing imported birds from Russia on Salisbury Plain.

mosquitoes: these insects feature in *The Wood Demon*. In Stanislavsky's 1899 production of *Uncle Vanya* at the Moscow Art Theatre, they reappeared with a vengeance (see p.li).

frozen, sick, and hungry men . . . to relieve their hunger and warm themselves: it would seem that the decline in the countryside bordering on ecological disaster has nothing to do with government policy or estate mismanagement but is to be blamed on the desire of the poor to cut timber for their home fires in order to cook food. It has certainly been brought on by 'the unequal struggle for existence' but not, surely, solely for the reasons Astrov suggests.

37 *It's to do with my stepdaughter*: Yelena is hardly being discreet as she promised Sonya, who would no doubt be mortified if she could hear.

(takes his hand): the stage direction is slightly ambiguous as the word for 'hand' and 'arm' are the same in Russian. If she takes his hand, the gesture would seem to be unambiguously 'forward'

and suggestive on Yelena's part. If she takes his arm, the
gesture is less forward and intimate and more urgently
remonstrative. Translators (and translations) vary between
'hand' and 'arm' but the distinction is important.

38 *silky-smooth ferret*: 'a fluffy weasel' in the original. Both are
predatory rodents except that the weasel is wild and the ferret
is used by humans to hunt other wild creatures.
(laughs through his teeth): the direction contains a suggestion
of unpleasantness and faint animality, although the animal
imagery has been attributed by Astrov to Yelena.
She tries to go. He bars her way: depending on the way this
scene is interpreted there is a possibility that this might be
performed as attempted assault.

39 *Lays her head on Astrov's chest*: the man's sexual urgency is
contagious; it is not that Yelena is flirtatious or has been
playing hard to get.
(with ill-grace): 'budiruia'. English translations offer different
stage directions preceding this speech ranging from 'with
bravado', to 'with false nonchalance', or 'inwardly fuming'. A
very recent translation has 'unabashed'. A literal translation of
'budiruia' would be 'sulkily'.
(Rolls the map into a tube): one imagines the sexual symbolism
is meant to be comic.

40 *I must be away from here today!*: Yelena's wish to leave may
be seen as a compound of shame and fear of her own
awakened desires.
Twenty-six enormous rooms: the house is clearly a very large
one; the family is small and, as there appear not to be many
servants, most of the rooms must be empty or unused.
Sonya!: there is a stage direction missing before, in the original,
the professor calls his daughter's name a second time: '*Sonya
does not hear him and stands with her head bowed sadly*'.
Marina sits down and knits a stocking: 'Like Yefim with his
tapping, she has a characteristic activity: she knits a stocking.
In these times of symbol-freighted criticism, our deduction
mechanism whisks us towards Clotho, the Fate who weaves'
(Albert Bermel, op. cit., p.52). 'The Nurse sits down and "*knits
a stocking*" like a revolutionary waiting to watch heads roll at
the guillotine' (Styan, 1971, p.127).
Lend me your ears: a reference to Mark Antony's oration over
the corpse of Julius Caesar in Shakespeare's play: 'Friends,

Romans, countrymen. Lend me your ears!'. This substitutes for
the expression which Serebryakov uses: 'Suspend your ears, so
to speak, from the nail of attentiveness.'

41 *A little unfriendly, your manner*: the translator has added this
phrase to explain the fact that Vanya responds to the professor
in unfamiliar fashion as 'you', having been addressed as 'thou'
by Serebryakov.

*I have asked you to come here today ... the Inspector-General
is on his way*: Serebryakov is in unusually playful mood and
pretends he is the mayor in Gogol's *The Government Inspector*
(1836), who opens the play with this line addressed to the
town officials.

manet omnes una nox: in Latin in the original where it is not,
as here, translated. The quotation is from the Roman lyric poet
and satirist, Horace (65–8 BC), from one of his four books of
Odes, in this case Book I, ode 28, l.15. It refers to what the
twentieth-century detective fiction writer, Raymond Chandler,
called 'The Big Sleep' – the permanently long night which
awaits us all.

My own life is over: a recurring refrain of the play uttered by
both old and young.

42 *within reasonable distance of St Petersburg*: see A Note on the
Translation, p.lxxxvii.

My late father: it has been suggested by some critics that this
is a play about 'fatherlessness' (bezotsovshchina), which was
the title of the very first full-length play Chekhov wrote.

under Turkish law: under which women are barred from
inheriting property.

Jean, il ne faut pas le contredire: French in the original. 'Jean,
you mustn't contradict him.'

43 *My brother's wife's brother*: Telegin names them both in the
original; the brother is Grigori Ilich and the wife's brother is
Konstantin Trofimovich Lakedemonov (a comical, highfalutin
name with classical Greek connotations).

I worked like an ox for ten years: presumably it is the estate
workers who worked like oxes while Vanya kept the accounts.

44 *a normal life ... Schopenhauer ... Dostoevsky*: both Arthur
Schopenhauer, the German philosopher (1788–1860), and the
Russian novelist, Fedor (Fyodor) Dostoevsky (1821–81), led
difficult and unhappy lives. The irony of considering 'normal'
the first, who was a philosophical pessimist, and the second, a
religiously tormented epileptic, is clear.

45 *Mother . . . Mother!*: Vanya uses the diminutive 'matushka'
   which seems incongruous when applied to a woman without
   any obvious maternal attributes.
46 *Nanna! Nanna!*: Sonya also uses a diminutive form,
   'nianechka'. At this moment of crisis, both turn for comfort to
   mother figures.
   you poor orphan child: Marina seems to recognise that Sonya
   seems 'fatherless' although, strictly speaking of course, she is
   not an orphan.
   lime tea, or raspberry: Marina's homely cure for all complaints.
   '"A cup of lime-flower water, or raspberry tea, and it will
   pass . . .". The phrase summarizes her ancient and apathetic
   view of these "children" and their problems. For Marina [. . .]
   everyone else is a child who has yet to grow up and learn
   acquiescence' (Styan, 1971, pp.130–1).
   Bang!: Vanya seems to be playing a child's game of cowboys
   and Indians where the uttered sound is a substitute for the real
   thing. However, this game is being played with live
   ammunition. 'What killer at large ever said "Bang!"? Like a
   child, Uncle Vanya is over-dramatizing a moment of which
   perhaps he has dreamed since he first saw Serebryakov for
   what he was' (Styan, 1971, p.131).
   Another botch-up?: see A Note on the Translation, p.lxxxvi
   and Translator's Introduction, p.lxxix. The idea of missing the
   professor twice may have derived from a moment in Act Four
   of *The Wood Demon* when Fedor Orlovski recounts a hunting
   episode to Serebryakov: 'Once I was coming back from a hunt
   and saw a tawny owl sitting on a tree . . . I take a pot shot at
   him! He doesn't budge . . . I bang a number nine at him . . .
   He still doesn't budge . . . Nothing moves him. He just sits and
   blinks.'

Act Four

48 *It serves both as his bedroom and as the estate office . . . a
   somewhat smaller table for Astrov*: with twenty-six rooms to
   choose from, there seems little reason why a single room
   should be quite so overcrowded. Telegin and Marina also
   choose this place to wind wool in, which seems incongruous.
   However, there is the suggestion that they are keeping an eye
   on Vanya, who tells them later to leave the room as he 'can't
   bear being watched over' (p.49).

a mat ... to prevent the peasants dirtying the floor: peasants were expected to stand in the doorway and not enter the room.
Only a little bit left: in view of the fact that people are said to be leaving, this could be a comment on the play itself: 'Nearly the end ...'
They just weren't fated to ... Predestined not to: this line may lend weight to those who see Marina as a figure of the mythological Fates who spun the thread of a person's life, cutting it to signify death.
Yes, it was a regular field of battle: see A Note on the Translation, p.lxxxvi). I.K. Aivazovsky (1817–1900) was a painter of seascapes.

49 *'Living on their charity!'*: it was not unusual for the nineteenth-century Russian landed gentry to have a permanent house-guest, someone usually of their own class who had, for one reason or another, fallen on hard times. Turgenev wrote a play *The Parasite* on precisely this theme.
we're none of us sitting idle, we're all of us working: again, the issue is raised about the relationship between 'idleness' and 'work'.

51 *another thirteen years to go*: the sense of something to be endured rather than something to be lived is all-pervasive.
when we're lying in our graves we might have pleasant dreams: anticipates Sonya's final speech.

52 *Enduring ... enduring ... endure ... Endure ... Endure!*: it seems painfully ironic that Vanya responds to this appeal to 'endure' rather than to 'live'.
work, something to do, otherwise I can't go on: work is here defined as a distraction, something just to fill in time.
(Sorts agitatedly through the papers): a desperate surrogate for real work.
Now I can be off, then. (Enter Yelena): a wonderfully ironic juxtaposition.

53 *to think better of me*: Yelena is concerned that Astrov think well of her when there is every reason for her to think ill of him.
Kursk: a town in Russia about 150 miles north of Kharkov.
decayed estates à la Turgenev: a reference to Turgenev's novella *Dvorianskoe gnezdo* (A Nest of Gentlefolk or A Nest of the Gentry, 1859).

54 *infected us all ... sow destruction*: it's ironic that Yelena

should be accused of destructiveness when in Act One she accuses everyone else of it.

Finita la commedia!: Italian in the original. 'The play (or comedy) is over!'

I'll take this pencil: commentators have made much of the sexual symbolism of this action.

they both at once move quickly apart: as well as the fear of discovery, this says much about the general fear of emotional involvement which seems to characterise just about everyone in the play and which might also be described as 'fear of life itself'.

55 *in these few short hours*: this suggests that the action is on the evening of the same day as Act Three.

He and Vanya kiss three times: the irony of this is apparent given Vanya's murderous intentions a few hours earlier.

pleasure of your company ... respect ... respect: we can assume that the professor means nothing of the kind but that if he knew of Astrov's 'impulsiveness and enthusiasm' via-à-vis Yelena, he might be less polite.

General farewells: 'obshchi poklon' suggests a single deep bow directed at all and sundry by the professor alone.

56 *Kisses him on the head*: like a child.

Work, work! (Rummages among the papers...): a repetition of Sonya's earlier pointless activity.

57 *people sending round a second time for their accounts*: it looks, rather oddly, as if it is not they who owe money but that those who owe them money are requesting invoices for the sums owed, and not for the first time.

I could just drop off now: Marina uses a nursery word 'bain'ka'. 'I feel like going bye-byes.'

Puts the maps away: this, combined with his clearing of his paints earlier, is the real sign that he is keeping his promise to Yelena, departing for good and forsaking the monthly pleasure of visiting the estate and indulging his favourite hobby.

two hundred and seventy-five roubles: if this is just one outstanding amount and the others are in any way similar, the estate is owed a tidy sum, all of which suggests that matters may have been being neglected long before the arrival of the professor and his wife. Richard Peace suggests, 'The estate accounts appear to have received little attention since early spring; they are for commodities purchased for Lent' (Peace, 1983, p.69).

58 *Thank you for having me here*: in the original he thanks them for 'the bread and salt' – traditional marks of Russian hospitality.

in Africa here the heat must be terrible: 'when the doctor, after a long pause, speaks of the heat of Africa, I shook with excitement in face of your talent and out of fear for people, for our colourless, miserable life' (Gorky in a letter to Chekhov, 20/30 November 1898). An entire continent is made to serve the speaker's need to fill a space between a request for a glass of vodka and its consumption.

You should have a morsel of bread with it, though: some commentators have noted the significance of Astrov's drinking vodka on its own without any accompanying food – the sure sign of an alcoholic to a Russian.

59 *He sits down by the door and quietly strums his guitar*: in fact, in the original, he 'quietly tunes his guitar' (nastraivaet gitaru). This could be an important distinction since tuning could possibly undercut the first half of Sonya's speech, even if done quietly.

What can we do, though?: much has been written about Sonya's final speech by commentators who either define the mood as optimistic, heroic, stoic, even tragic, as opposed to those who see it as pessimistic, religiose, maudlin and bathetic. J.L. Styan has made a list of the pros and cons: 'Magarshack's characterization of the speech as one of faith and courage ignores the ironies an audience readily perceives. For political, religious or philosophical reasons, critical opinion has been sharply divided on the issue, and I owe to J.J. Moran a "poll" of critics who interpret Sonya's optimism literally and those who do not.' He then lists the names of ten literalists and sixteen non-literalists (Styan, 1971, p.141). It also raises the question of Chekhov's own religious beliefs. His father was an intensely religious person and Chekhov was brought up within the Orthodox faith, signs of which are detectable throughout his life. His letters contain many religious references and show evidence of his special feeling for the Easter period of the Christian calendar. However, during the last four years of his life he declared, 'I am not a religious person' (letter to Menshikov of 28 January 1900), and in another letter (to Diaghilev of 12 July 1903) he wrote: 'I can only regard with bewilderment an educated man who is also religious.'

Telegin quietly plays his guitar: what does Telegin play at this juncture? Is it a doleful accompaniment to the second half of Sonya's speech or, repeating the end of Act One, is it a polka? If the latter, then this is no longer an accompaniment but in ironic juxtaposition to the speech.

60 *We shall rest!*: the verb is 'otdokhnut', the root of which is 'dukh' (breath) and 'otdykh' (a break, a rest, or a holiday). The sense of the verb is to 'take a breather' or 'we'll have time to breathe'. There is a possible irony here in the anticipation that, once placed in a coffin and sunk in the ground, they will be able to breathe. The most significant accompanying sound, as the curtain falls, is then the one made by the watchman (as if knocking in the nails), while Telegin strums on his guitar and Maria Vasilyevna and Marina engage in the inconsequential activities of margin-jotting and needle-clicking. *Marina winds her wool*: in fact she is described in the original as performing the same activity as at the beginning of Act One: 'Marina viazhet chulok' (Marina knits a stocking).

Questions for Further Study

1. 'Why write about someone who goes off to the North Pole while their grief-stricken lover throws herself from a belfry. Life isn't like that' (Anton Chekhov). What are the implications of this statement for an understanding of *Uncle Vanya*?

2. *Uncle Vanya* has been described as a tragedy, a comedy, a farce, a melodrama and even as a version of the Italian comedy of masks, *commedia dell'arte*. What genre, or mixture of genres, do you think the play belongs to and why?

3. How successful is Chekhov in making boredom an interesting dramatic subject in *Uncle Vanya*?

4. Gorky saw Chekhov as a moralist, the moral of his writing being an indictment of the way his characters lead their lives, 'You live badly, ladies and gentlemen'. Does *Uncle Vanya* seem to you to bear out Gorky's view or is 'the moralist' conspicuous by his absence from this play?

5. How are love themes handled in *Uncle Vanya*?

6. A recent critic has described the main theme of *Uncle Vanya* as the clash between creative and destructive impulses. How far would you agree?

7. Consider the theme of 'frustration' in *Uncle Vanya*.

8. In what ways does the past impact upon the present in *Uncle Vanya*?

9. To what extent is *Uncle Vanya* a play in which symbolic elements are important?

10. How is the notion of 'work' treated in *Uncle Vanya*?

11. The minor characters in *Uncle Vanya* have been described as 'choric figures'. What do you understand by this and how would you assess their place in the play?

12. The rural setting of Chekhov's plays usually establishes analogies between the worlds of nature and that of human beings. To what extent is this true of *Uncle Vanya* and what are the implications of such links?

13. Consider the significance of 'time' in *Uncle Vanya*.

14. Consider the theme of 'waste' in *Uncle Vanya*.

15. Chekhov is always being complimented on the qualities of his 'subtext', i.e. that which is subtly revealed about character and situation below the surface of what is actually being said. To what extent is 'subtext' an important element in *Uncle Vanya*?

16. To what extent do you think *Uncle Vanya* is a 'timeless' play or one with specific links to a particular historical moment?

17. How important is the representation of the connection between childhood and adulthood in *Uncle Vanya*?

18. Consider the significance of symmetry in *Uncle Vanya* in, for example, its structural organisation and its 'pairing' of characters and scenes.

19. In what ways does the conclusion to Act Four of *Uncle Vanya* relate to the whole of the play?

20. Basing your opinion on the accounts of productions as different as those of Stanislavsky and Nekrosius, what kind of production do you think would best serve the play and why?

21. Discuss the theme of 'arrival and departure' in *Uncle Vanya* and how 'exits and entrances' might contribute to an appreciation of this aspect of the play.